Lay of the Land

Reflections on Life in Rural Ireland

RED STAG

Fiona O'Connell

Published in 2019 by:
RED STAG
(a Mentor Books imprint)

Mentor Books Ltd
43 Furze Road
Sandyford Industrial Estate
Dublin 18
Republic of Ireland

Tel: +353 1 295 2112 / 3
Fax: +353 1 295 2114
Email: admin@mentorbooks.ie
Website: www.mentorbooks.ie

A CIP catalogue record for this title is available from the British Library.
ISBN 978-1-912514-47-2

Cover image: Dana Winder
www.danawinder.com

Illustrations: Caroline Barry
@otherworldceramics

Visit our website: **www.mentorbooks.ie**

Author's Note

I started to write a weekly column, which I called 'Lay of the Land, ' in *The Sunday Independent* in 2012. As the title suggests, it began as a series of reflections on the natural world. But 'lay of the land' also means to say things as they are, and this dual aspect adds potency. For the actuality of rural life often negates the romanticism.

On that note, I was born in the city but consider myself less of a blow-in than a country person who finally made it home. Certainly, I have always felt more comfortable when close to nature. My father's rural roots instilled a yearning in me for the land; visiting relatives down tree-lined avenues in Ireland's lush midlands fed this desire for a wilder world.

Though growing up in a Dublin suburb was not the same as it is today. My generation was perhaps the last to live in a city that still had green spaces, with hedgehogs and badgers roaming the fields around our new estate that was steadily swallowing up their habitat.

Indeed, the elusive notion of 'land' has forced me to ask myself some fundamental questions. Because what do we mean by the 'land of Ireland'? Do we mean land as God gave it to us? Or land that our ancestors foraged before they cleared and planted it, and raised livestock on it? Land as property? Land as raw material for agribusiness?

Or do we mean land as recreation, or place of renewal and retreat? Land as the home of poets? Land as the fount of legend, seat of the sacred?

The concept of land is as complex as that of time, which witnesses and wields changes to the land and those who live on it. Perhaps that is why land, in the sense of the natural world, is so infinitely precious. The people of this former 'land of saints and scholars' viewed it as a conduit to the divine.

The many pasts that have played out on this land have left their traces on it. They provide perspective on the present, through their treasure trove of crumbling castles, their customs and folklore that still influence us.

My love of the land grew as I did into adulthood. Till finally, prompted by a friend who had already upped sticks for the sticks, I broke for the border

– or the provincial paradise that lies beyond the pale. And though I retain a soft spot for 'the Big Smoke', I have never felt more at home than I do living far from the one where I was born.

For we are constantly told that cities are scintillating hubs of excitement and adventure. Yet nothing compares to an unexpected encounter with wildlife, or mist rising off the land, which changes with the shifting seasons. The sassy shopkeeper with a bullshit bag pinned on the wall, or honesty sheds guarded by camera-shy collies, or a farmer who retired not just herself but also her herd of cows.

'Lay of the Land' is at times a labour of love for those who never had their say: the County Home boys and the 'difficult' girls who were locked up in laundries, mothers burdened by too many mouths to feed or the many that were forced to leave these shores.

And then there are all those who live on the land. Not just us humans, but also the flora and fauna, the worm as well as the early bird that catches it, the foxglove and the fox. For these too are part of the great hidden web of life and death that binds what we call the land of Ireland.

This is why 'Lay of the Land' is almost a weekly wrestling match with a presence that refuses to be pinned down. Nothing is quite as it seems, for what at first can appear physically stable, presenting itself from afar as a quiet field, close up turns out to be as busy as a beehive. Not only that, but a field can change and be changed: from tillage to grass or sold as a site for housing.

Every week I try to look at some tiny part of this rich web, hoping with words to make a few strands vibrate so that readers can share with me what I see and feel.

That is why I offer this collection with humility, knowing that many of you see further and feel more deeply than I do. And I am glad of that because without you, there would be no one to stand watch over the Lay of the Land.

Dedication

In memory of my beautiful brother, Michael, who lived up to a book he once gave me called *What Matters Most Is How Well You Walk Through the Fire*. And for my beloved parents, Anne and Paul.

Acknowledgements

To Daniel McCarthy and everyone at Red Stag, especially Treasa O'Mahony for her skills, wit and understanding.

Sincere thanks to all at the *Sunday Independent*, in particular Shane Fitzsimons and Campbell Spray for their great expertise and kindness.

Thanks to Anne Harris for liking the idea of 'Lay of the Land' enough to give me the gig. And to Eoghan Harris for always believing in my writing and being so generous with his guidance.

So much thanks to the good people of Thomastown for making me feel so welcome.

Thanks to John Fitzgerald for the great stories. Special thanks to the inspirational Caroline Barry for the stunning illustrations. And Dana Winder for hopefully making people judge this book by her beautiful cover. Enormous gratitude to all the people who read my column every week. And to those who have trusted me with their tales and thoughts.

Thanks to all my family and friends who have given me their support over the years. Especially thanks to Ian, my fearless, funny and gorgeous good man, for putting up with me and giving so much of his time and energy to helping with the mammoth task of selecting pieces to include in this book.

CONTENTS

SPRING

SUMMER

AUTUMN

WINTER

SPRING

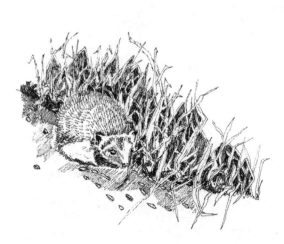

This prickly customer deserves our consideration

When does an animal lover not love seeing an animal? When it's a hedgehog during the day, especially on the road, because usually it means they are dead.

And since March marks the end of hedgehog hibernation, their massacre is set to begin again.

Though seeing a squashed hedgehog when I was a child growing up in Dublin was hardly news. Indeed, it was so common that the phrase became a humorous way to describe something that happens with mundane frequency.

I laughed too, without registering the reality behind the wisecracking; little critters were being crushed in such numbers that it was a bad joke.

The mowing-down of these uncuddly yet cute creatures started in the Seventies, with the increase in traffic on Irish roads. The plight of the prickly ones was compounded by the building boom, with ever more being evicted from their habitats as the fields surrounding our house were turned into suburbs. Hedgehogs became frequent visitors to our back garden, which had in fact once been their home.

Ironically, hedgehogs are often safer in cities, especially in residential areas where speed bumps work in their favour. I see far too many of their battered bodies here in the countryside, where drivers tend to tear along.

And you can't blame the hedgehog; he was doing perfectly well just as he was for aeons. It's hardly fair to expect him to suddenly evolve a supersonically fast shuffle because we moved the goalposts.

We may wonder why the chicken crossed the road, but the hedgehog takes that risk because he has to, travelling up to 3km per night in his forage for food.

I pulled over one evening last year when I spotted the latest casualty in my headlights. The hedgehog was dead, though perfectly intact, perhaps belted by a passing car and then dying from internal injuries.

At least it gave me the chance to study him up close. And what a revelation it was to examine his intricate features. This humble hedgehog had a face like a hobbit. He wore an expression that reminded me of Yoda, the wise old Grand Master of the Jedi Order in *Star Wars*.

I moved his body from the middle of the road that he never managed to cross, to hibernation under a pile of leaves in the shelter of the forest. His rest would last forever, instead of just the winter.

Hedgehogs are supposed to be a protected species. Surely it wouldn't burst the bank to put up some road signs, especially around wooded areas and hedgerows, asking drivers to take care especially at night, and also during their mating season in August.

Otherwise we are like the cyborgs in the *Terminator* movies; merciless machines crushing the life out of less infallible creatures.

A little field fever can bring home the bacon

The Bull McCabe had better move over – 'field fever' is not confined to the fictional world of brilliant Irish playwright John B Keane.

I was reminded of this by a woman who moved from the centre of this country town to a cottage on its outskirts last year, for the sake of the acre-sized plot that came with it.

She plans to use it to start a fruit and vegetable business. And a pair of pedigree pigs are helping her reach that goal. She acquired her porky partners after a farmer who promised to plough the field did not come through.

'I waited all summer and nothing happened. So I thought, "You know what? I can buy two pigs and they'll do the same job". '

This 'waste not, want not' woman used the floorboards that she saved from her old house to make their enclosure. She moves it once the pigs have turned over that patch of earth. It's 'quite an ordeal' to dismantle and put together again, but worth the effort. 'They take off the top layer and all I have to do is clean up the sod a bit. They're going to dig the whole lot up for me.'

The Gloucester Old Spots in question are heritage hogs, though this commerically-minded carnivore views them primarily as 'lovely meat'. They are multi-tasking their little trotters off for her, making the six-month-old siblings a moveable feast.

Talk about hogging the profits: once they are done digging for this 'Bella' McCabe, she won't so much be bringing home the bacon as taking the bacon from their home to have them butchered to make more money. No wonder she's having a field day.

'I don't like the thought of it,' she says. 'It's not that they're beautiful, but they're just so comical. I couldn't eat them, no way.'

But she's busy pursuing punters who are happy to pig out on them. 'There's interest but no one's committed quite yet.'

No wonder these sweet swines are making the most of their free-range but limited lives. Contrary to expectations, they proved on their arrival that they favour freedom over food.

'They legged it out of the trailer to the top of the field. The breeder said they'd just follow the bucket into the pen, but they didn't. They saw the field and ran.'

The pair only entered the enclosure much later, when they were cold and hungry.

'At that point I just thought: "OK, I don't mind eating you guys – at all!" But now I've got kind of fond of them.'

Fond enough to leave them a little patch of the field they'll have furrowed, to enjoy for the rest of their natural lives?

Because clearly it's not just people who fantasise about fields.

Political hopefuls go the whole hog for local support

How to save a set of sibling swine that face the pork chop is on my mind this month. Because, judging by the progress they're making ploughing the field for a fruit and vegetable gardener in this country town, they will soon be out of a job and inside a slaughterhouse.

But it's politics and not pigs that is preoccupying other locals this weather. For April showers aren't confined to rain: a plethora of politicians is floating around town, feverishly canvassing for the elections that take place next month. And hence making an almighty hullabaloo over any miscellaneous 'hoi polloi' they happen upon.

This method of currying political favour has been going on since before I was knee high to a grasshopper – or to one of these 'gunning to meet you' guys. They are eager to make physical contact with punters, as if playing that children's game of tag where you become 'it' if someone touches you.

Perhaps their topsy-turvy hope is that touching as many members of the

16

public as possible will turn them into 'it', as in the winning candidate.

Some were on the main street recently, hobnobbing to beat the band and shaking passing hands as if that would seal the democratic deal for them. They even wound their way into the butcher's, where they waylaid the beautiful blonde who wields a cleaver there, making her blush with their efforts to woo her.

Then there was a knock at my door the following morning. I presumed it was PJ the postman, who often raps on the window to wave bills and other documents of doom at me. Instead, I found canny independent candidate and local artist Ramie Leahy, looking dapper in an elegant ensemble. He appeared appalled by my own 'at-home' garb of 'Sloppy Joes'.

'I'm just up,' I made an excuse. But since it wasn't the crack of dawn, this seemed to appal him even more. Or maybe he was practising his 'concerned citizen' expression.

'I'm doing this the democratic way,' he declared. 'Very few people know you can run for local election by paying a stipend of €100 – or alternatively by getting 15 assenters. It's not published – do you ever hear about it on radio or TV?'

So has he found 'A Few Good Men', plus 12 angry ones, to make up the magic number to back his bid for the ballot box?

'I have indeed,' he laughs. 'They're in this brown envelope!'

Leahy lives in Dysart, the birthplace of George Berkeley, where a family of potbellied pigs roam free. So I ask him the burning question: can he offer two swine sanctuary?

'Not a chance,' he says. 'My lot would kill them – it's their turf.'

No wonder George Orwell made pigs the political leaders in *Animal Farm*. It sounds like they have a lot in common.

There's no ducking out of this Easter Rising

Easter eggs will be everywhere this day next week. But a few might turn up early in my backyard, in a scenario that proves fairy tales are based on facts.

However, the same could be said of all fiction – especially when it focuses on our fondness for fantasy. Certainly, there was no shortage of Walter Mitty types canvassing during the recent election. And plenty of them can be found all year round in any Irish country town, labouring under illusions of grandeur and importance – whether as artists, oracles of wisdom or supreme shakers and makers – a reality existing entirely within their egos.

However, not just human beings but honking beings can be guilty of megalomania – as illustrated by this tale with an ironic twist on *The Ugly Duckling*.

Once upon a time – last winter, to be precise – ducks started visiting the riverbank beneath this town cottage in search of sustenance. Some stood far from the mallard crowd, bobbing their heads to catch my attention – like cute children who stay still in a noisy group to get noticed. They scored food with their bulls-eye beaks, displaying impressive dexterity. (Or 'ducksterity'?)

Eventually some took to waddling around the backyard. At first it was amusing to see them ambling about. But talk about an overdose of duck surprise. Because as Basil says in the Gourmet Night episode of *Fawlty Towers*, 'If you don't like duck, then you're rather stuck.'

For their D-day landing has turned into a full-blown invasion, meaning I've discovered their dark side – not so much Darth Vader as Duck Vader.

I'd almost prefer the Donald – as in that risible but dangerous republican candidate in the USA – than the many Donald Ducks outside.

It's not that I'm less fond of these fowl. But I do detest cleaning up their deposits. Or seeing the songbirds go hungry as they hoover up the seed with their boisterous beaks. For now they're so bountiful that my backyard is like duck soup – and I'm the noodle.

They're driving me daffy. I shoo them away, ruffling many a fine feather as they fly off with a haughty honk or querulous quack, only to duck back within minutes.

But here's the bit that quacks me up, considering that The Ugly Duckling is the tale of a swan who is born into a family of ducks that cast him out because he clearly doesn't belong. Apparently one solution to my duck uprising is to get a life-size statue of a swan.

Other options include hanging bright objects like CDs on a string; maybe something by Ducky Gillespie?

And I'm not joking about Easter coming early.

Because I've noticed a duo of Daphne ducks waddling under the oil tank, making me wonder if they are nesting.

I certainly won't be egging them on.

I'm not sure my mother knows me anymore

Modern life has been so hijacked by commerical interests that we now endure a not-so-merry-go-round of relentless red letter days – each one presented as an absolute imperative that cannot be ignored.

Now Mother's Day is here. But while we may 'bah humbag' some over-hyped holidays, most of us won't turn a blind eye to this particular tradition.

Which is why mothers all around this country town today are being mollycoddled – or at least made to grin and bear the somewhat dubious pleasure of breakfast in bed, courtesy of their amateur chef children.

Which may make it necessary to treat those same mothers to lunch or dinner in rural restaurants and hotels that will be delighted to make up for those earlier burnt offerings.

Meanwhile, former city slickers, such as yours truly, will have to get on their bikes (or rather, get in their bangers) and head back to 'the Big Smoke' to do likewise.

I always bring flowers whenever I visit, because I know my mother loves them – though she no longer tells me so. Just as she won't understand why I've brought an extra big bouquet today. For my mother has frontal lobe dementia.

Her decline was slow and almost imperceptible, but in hindsight there were signs – like the way she started repeating the end of sentences.

Perhaps it was harder to detect because my mother was always shy and introverted. Though as a singer who performed in the chorus of operas at the Gaiety Theatre and at Feis Ceoils around the country, she also loved the limelight.

But, gradually, it became clear that something was seriously wrong. The various vile dementias have distinct features. Frontal lobe is characterised by a lack of emotion and loss of empathy – meaning you could tell my mother that you had just been in a car crash and she wouldn't react.

Most likely, the dementia was triggered by my younger brother's sudden death.

Of course, losing a child doesn't at all necessarily lead to losing your mind, but trauma seems to lie behind many incidences of this devastating disease.

I'm not sure she recognises me anymore.

Sometimes she says she loves me – but the black humour that accompanies such tragedies means she is inclined to tell complete strangers on the street that same good news. She seems happy to see me – but not for long, preferring photographs of us when we were young children.

But there is another photograph that my mother holds dear, of another precious lost child called Madeline McCann. So maybe dementia has not entirely conquered her, at least when it comes to feeling for another mourning mother.

Mother's Day occurs just once a year, but a mother loves as long as she lives.

And even when a child is gone, that love is not.

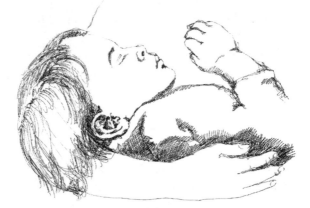

March comes in like a lion and out like a lamb

It's March, and spring lambs are frolicking in green fields, reminding me that when March 'comes in like a lion, it goes out like a lamb.' This month should live up to that, with the unveiling of the next Catholic representative of the Lamb of God.

Pope Benedict XVI's resignation came as a shock to many. Much like my shock when I discovered that my grandfather was actually Pope Paul VI.

The misunderstanding was due to an ornamental plate that hung in my grandparents' home. The man painted on it was the spit of my grandfather. It was only later, when I saw a photograph of his pious doppelganger, that the penny dropped.

Though my grandfather was a devout Catholic, sometimes my Protestant grandmother would tag along when he went to Mass. The significance of the smouldering incense literally went over her head. But she still enjoyed Pope John Paul II's visit to Ireland. Like her, he had lived through World War Two. Which brings to mind a story from the Martin Gilbert book *The Holocaust*.

It concerns the winter of 1942, when Jewish parents were forced to make agonising choices as the Nazis were sweeping through the ghettos of Poland.

In desperation, Moses and Helen Hiller carried their baby to the home of family friends, a childless Catholic couple named Jachowicz. They begged them to take the child and gave them the address of family in Washington. Then they were deported to Auschwitz.

The war ended, but like most Jews the Hillers didn't return. Their blue-eyed boy was now four and believed he was a Catholic, and the Jachowiczes' child.

Finally the Jachowiczes decided to baptize him. They went to the nearest church in the village of Wadowice, where a young priest was completing his training. But before the rite, Mrs Jachowicz confessed.

The priest listened and then asked: 'What do you think the boy's parents would want you to do?'

This devoted Catholic woman was honest. She said: 'I don't have to imagine. I know. I will never forget. My friend, Helen Hiller, giving the last look on her baby, which was in my arms, and she said to me: "In case, God forbid, that we will not come back, please, do all the efforts to give Shachne back into Jewish arms".'

Rev Karol Wojtyla was gentle but firm. He would not baptize the child.

Almost 50 later, he confirmed his knowledge of the fact that the boy had made it to America, where he became an observant Jew.

That priest showed himself to be gentle as a lamb in the practise of his beliefs, and worthy to become Pope John Paul II.

Tales of frantic feeding, both fowl and fair

It's only early March, and there are still many mightily cold and frosty days left in the spring mix. Maybe that's why the splendidly intricate spider webs which usually run along the railings of the bridge in this country town are long gone.

So I'm frantically feeding as many of our feathered friends as I can. Though it has to be said that I do so all year, as I reckon their ever-diminishing habitats necessitate it.

However, it's not just birds, but bigger beaks too that are begging for sustenance. For friendly local fowl are devouring any delicacies they can get.

It started a few months ago, when I noticed ducks waddling around by my bird tables, which are situated on a grassy terrace above the river. They were busily hoovering up dropped seeds, as well as poking around the roots of the willows, possibly searching for hibernating insects.

Some are the ducklings that hatched in the yard of what was then an empty house across the road, from where we managed to escort them safely to the river.

It's a case of feast or famine for these well-loved fowl. People feed them bread during the summer when insects are everywhere and they need it least. But there are few visitors to the river's edge when the weather turns wintry.

Which is actually a blessing in disguise. Because white bread, in particular, is dastardly for ducks.

Not many people know this. I only found out last year that, far from being a ducky do-gooder by dishing out dough, I was doing the ducks no favours at all.

But ducks are discerning when given the chance. As I discovered, once I began throwing a few handfuls of seeds their way. Because the ducks went demented for it.

Soon, if I even appeared in the yard, let alone approached the steps to the bird feeds, ducks from far down the other side of the river would spot me, heralding the news with a host of happy honks.

A chorus of quacks then told me that they were on their way, with more than a dozen ducks dashing like a platoon of old fashioned flying machines across the river, to make their charmingly comical landing: legs akimbo, orange webbed feet splayed, followed by a stupendous splash.

Then up the bank they advance, as more reinforcements land behind them. Talk about a D-Day landing.

Others approach from under the bridge, waddling on their merry mallard way. Once they see me scattering seed and the other ducks digging in, they want to get a move on.

Being a duck, there is no question of breaking into a stylish sprint or a graceful gallop. For the Great Creator decided to give us all a break, no matter how hard a day we're having, by making a duck simply waddle faster.

Of which, it must be said, there are surely few sights more endearing.

Certainly, it never fails to 'quack' me up.

I finally know why the freed bird can sing

It's three years today since I started writing this column, with a piece about refugees of a feathered kind; two budgerigars who came to live with me after they were abandoned in my late brother's workplace.

These seemingly inconsequential creatures were once popular pets, for I regularly meet people who had one as a child. They invariably relate how the bird soon died, either from the loneliness of life cooped up in a cage, with perhaps a plastic bird acting as a pathetic placebo for a mate, or by flying out an open window.

For budgerigars originally hail from Down Under, so escapees have a hard time finding birds of a feather with which to flock together. Instead of fat cats relishing the prospect of getting more than cream.

For 11 years, those beautiful birdbrains ruined my TV viewing, chirping and squawking at the sound, which seemed to trigger an instinctual memory of when they lived in noisy flocks.

If I turned up the volume, they gamely followed suit. Despite her delicate appearance, the lemony hen in particular could honk for Ireland.

They were lucky to have each other. But the male had a bee in his brightly coloured bonnet. He would mutter sourly back at me through the bars, as if angry with his lot.

Who could blame him? The people who dumped him probably shouted the prattling pair into silence before putting them through a bumpy bus ride into the city and life in a cage on top of a filing cabinet. A plastic red rose made their prison look pretty, but their lives no more lovely.

I bought a swing, which the green-and-yellow fellow took to rocking on grimly, hunched over and still bellyaching. Finally I opened the cage door – and discovered that they had never flown before, as they sat looking out, unsure what to do.

But you know what they say about a will finding a way. I bird-proofed my home and established an open door policy. Never once after they flew did the male bird use the swing again. And they found their voice – with a vengeance, emitting thrilling new sounds.

I Know Why The Caged Bird Sings is the poignant title of Maya Angelou's autobiography. Well, I think I know why the free bird does. Because it's fun.

Their end came soon after I moved to the country, with the lemony hen passing first.

Her loyal mate spent his final months among a colony of his own. Where, true to his nature, he took on the role of elder lemon, escorting chicks to the food and water stations.

Luckily, there is no shortage of their species around me in this country town. A visitor from Dublin once exclaimed that there was an escaped pet bird outside.

I looked at the green finch on the feeder with a smile and remembered my feathered friends; now faraway but free forever.

Contrasting city and country encounters

Sometime's it's not the experience of city and country life that differ, so much as the details.

Years ago now, thankfully, back when I was living in 'the Big Smoke' , I was walking up a city centre street with a male friend, when we heard people running behind us.

I immediately felt uneasy, though ostensibly there should be nothing particularly sinister about the sound of footsteps. But sometimes paranoia is proved right.

We came to a halt as a gang of teenage boys blocked our path and surrounded us. My first real inkling of fear came when I looked into the eyes of the ringleader and sensed he did not recognise us as fellow beings.

Sure enough, one of them grabbed my umbrella and started using it to whack my friend, while another moved in to land a headbutt.

At that point, we somehow managed to break away. We hurried on – shaken, and stirred enough to tell a garda we encountered what had happened.

I had a similarly unexpected encounter with a bunch of buckos soon after I moved to the country. It occurred in one of my favourite places to go for a walk, where fields bordered by virgin forest lead down to the same river that runs past my town cottage.

I had made a few attempts at feeding the 12 horses that live there. But though a couple of them were curious enough to approach and sniff the proffered carrots, they didn't really seem to know what to do.

For my part, I also found the experience a little daunting. These huge horses were nervy and clearly unused to people. It made sense when I learnt that they were rescues, being former hunting horses and cruelty cases.

I decided that it was best to admire them from afar. So I gave them a wide berth thereafter, though they always paused to glance at me when I passed.

Until, one day, they must have decided that it was time for more formal introductions.

I was making my way back up the trail to the gate, when I heard a sound behind me. Correction: I heard a stampede of hooves that sounded hot on my heels. I turned around and saw the 12 tearaways charging my way. No apocalyptic horsemen were needed for the situation to be intimidating.

They came to a halt on the grassy border, just inches from where I stood. There was a moment when nothing happened. Then the smallest of them, a ghostly white mare, stepped on to the trail and blocked my path.

She eyed me, as if saying 'well?' as people around these parts tend to greet each other. I glanced at her gang of galloping gee-gees, who were also watching. Then the pony stepped aside and I walked on.

Leaving me shaken once again by encountering sudden strangers. But this time stirred into wonder.

Sheepish secret that shaped Charlie Chaplin

I'm with George Bernard Shaw, who said 'animals are my friends…and I don't eat my friends'. But neither do I eat the head off carnivores – or those who supply their demands. Especially as one of the most decent landlords I ever had was a butcher.

Ireland is not a renter's paradise, and many of the property owners I leased from over the years were fairly horrible. But he was both a butcher and a gentleman. He'd always greet me, when I came downstairs from the flat above his premises, with a 'Morning, Fiona!' and a big, friendly smile – standing there all rosy-cheeked and cheerful, cleaver in hand and his apron splattered with blood.

I lived there for ages, despite the smell of raw meat that came up through the floorboards in summer. He is still carving up carcasses on Dublin's Wexford Street, and I still pop in for a chat if I'm in the city and passing.

The butchers in this country town seem likewise a lovely lot – unless you've got 'prime cut' printed across your person.

I often see a traffic cone set outside the adjoining abattoir when I'm on my way to pick up the *Sunday Independent*, the space occupied by a vehicle with a livestock trailer attached by the time I'm walking back.

Sometimes I watch as the animals are unloaded and corralled down the side entrance. It reminds me of the part in Charlie Chaplin's autobiography, where he pinpoints the defining moment of his life.

Chaplin often stayed with his aunt in the east end of London during his childhood, where there was an abattoir at the end of the road. One day, one of the sheep being herded to its death managed to escape.

It made a frantic bid for freedom down the crowded row of shops and houses, knocking over important-looking individuals. Grand-hatted dames collided bum-over-heel with pot-bellied businessmen in bowler hats. Fruit rolled everywhere, making people unwilling participants in the unfolding slapstick.

A delighted four-year-old Chaplin stood watching it all, laughing at the failed attempts of red-cheeked workers to catch the sheep, who kicked up its black hooves and valiantly resisted.

Until the inevitable happened, and the sheep was captured. It was held in a wrestler's grip until butchers in bloodied aprons came to claim it.

Only then did Chaplin realise the fate that awaited the fleecy fugitive who had caused so much fun.

Chaplin said that event crystallised the humour that he would go on to master.

Sometimes I remember him when I glimpse sheep between the trailer slats outside the abattoir. Life continues around them, as if everything is normal.

But a curtain is about to fall on those cowering creatures – like the one that signalled 'the end' in a silent movie.

Because rent is owing on use of their landlord's fields.

Surreal sight of solemn farewells to the Irish stoat

'Marry in May and rue the day,' goes the saying – though many make their vows in early summer and do very well in the happily ever after, directions to their big day displayed on telegraph poles around this country town.

Any why not? For death has dominion all-year round, with sad farewells taking place even when the sun shines, although humans are not unique in lamenting their loved ones, as the Irish stoat – which mates this season – reminds us.

This feisty little fellow is still sometimes referred to as a weasel in rural parts, although the only members of that species to be found in Ireland are either the human variety or the furry Frankenstein minks that escape from fur farms and wreak havoc on native wildlife.

But stoats are a long way from those negative associations, especially when it comes to showing solidarity with their brothers and sisters. Folk in the past knew not to attack one, for a shrill whistle would soon bring backup. The stoat would also follow you for miles, peering out from behind fences and hedges to make sure it kept you firmly in its sights.

Because if an elephant never forgets, these fierce fighters go one step further by using their excellent memory to get their own back. In ancient times these creatures were associated with the other world. It was said they would learn where you lived and then wait for a chance to exact revenge; such as killing every fowl or lamb on your farm.

Perhaps the most remarkable thing about this animal, that regularly targets prey more than twice its size, is its behaviour when bereaved. Many tales are told, similar to this one by a man who was heading home one moonlit night.

He was enjoying the calm of a country walk, when he suddenly noticed that the roadway ahead of him seemed to be undulating, the movement coming in a wave in his direction.

The hair on the back of his neck stood on end as he pressed himself against a tree by the side of the ditch. He heard the scratching sound of many nailed feet, with the odd squeal or hiss, and every so often a soft bark resounding in the night.

Then the scene turned truly surreal. For in front of the moving throng, four strong young stoats bore on high the body of the stoat king, his colouring silver-grey in the moonlight.

Without thinking, the man removed his cap and bowed his head in silent prayer while this strange funeral procession moved along within touching distance of his shoes.

Stoats of every sort and size passed, with some on either side and behind, keeping control and order among the mourning creatures.

The man strained his eyes to watch them leave the road and disappear through a gap to make their way across the fields towards high ground.

The scent of musk lingered in the night air, along with the realisation that all creatures have their customs and traditions as they face the trials and tribulations of all whose lives are ruled by time.

In praise of our brother and sister creatures

St Patrick's Day is over, and no one's decked out in green anymore. Except the 40 deepening shades in the fields, now that spring has truly arrived.

A love of nature was the reason I moved to the countryside. But animals are my great love, and there's no shortage of them here either. That's my bugbear with St Patrick. He meant well, but maybe by banishing snakes, he initiated the attitude that animals are dispensable when no longer pleasurable, or when it's profitable.

Fortunately, spring has brought us a new saint, thanks to our new Pope. In his choice of name, Pope Francis honours St Francis of Assisi, the patron saint of animals.

It's been argued that no one in history was as dedicated to imitating the life of Christ and carrying out his work as the founder of the Franciscan Order. Pope Francis is intent on following in his footsteps. So I look forward to seeing him raise awareness about our 'brother and sister creatures', as St Francis referred to animals.

St Francis also stated that 'not to hurt our humble brethren in fur, feather or fin, is our first duty to them, but to stop there is not enough. We have a higher mission; to be of service to them whenever they require it.' What would he make of this Christian country's track record with animal rights and animal welfare – whether in the form of pets, farm animals, sports or our seas?

Cardinal Brady says Pope Francis will reflect the merciful face of Christ to the world. He can expect an uphill battle, given his namesake's insight that 'if you have men who will exclude any of God's creatures from the shelter of compassion, you will have men who will deal likewise with their fellow men'.

Some people argue that those who care for animals must not care for people. Yet Martin Luther King, who was assassinated for championing civil rights, also believed that 'one day the absurdity of the almost universal human belief in the slavery of other animals will be palpable. We shall then have discovered our souls and become worthier of sharing this planet with them'.

St Francis of Assisi is my kind of Christian because he practised what he preached and made no exception to the rule of love for God's creatures.

That's why I'm following our new Pope's example and making St Francis the patron saint of 'Lay of the Land'. Hopefully, he'll help me sing the praises, and where necessary the pleas, of all sentient beings, like he literally did.

So I wish you a furry, feathered and finned day. No need to wear green; just be kind to kitty.

Horsing around is child's play for this couple

'April showers bring forth May flowers', goes the proverb. At least the 'Lay of the Land' isn't getting soaked in the city. Because watching concrete go *Fifty Shades of Grey* isn't very exciting.

Bad weather is better in the sticks. All you need is a pair of wellies, and you're free to hike through lush, green fields, rain dripping from the branches of majestic trees.

What metropolis can counter such rural charms? Not even London can compete with this particular country town, which boasts its very own Big Ben.

For that's the name of the white horse that lives across the river from me, with his sidekick pony pal. The horse hobbit has no name, so I've christened him Ben Beag. I suppose being the filly who feeds them could earn me the nickname Ben Her.

The two Bens may be an odd couple, but they're very much a pair. Often I see them grooming each other's flanks. At other times they touch necks, a graceful gesture that seems to reasure.

Maybe they need it. Rain or snow, cold or sunshine, they bear the elements in a field bordered by stone walls. In summer the apple trees provide shade, but this late spring the branches are bare.

Few cars passing on the bridge above notice these unexceptional equines. After all, they're not racehorses, stunning as supermodels and worth a bet.

But when the weather is good – and sometimes even when it's bad – these unassuming animals play host to an endless stream of visitors. In fact, I'm beginning to suspect that Big Ben is a reincarnation of a particularly charismatic pope.

People are forever offering their babies to him, as if to receive his blessing. All they need do is prop a toddler on the wall, and Big Ben will abandon whatever patch of grass he's nibbling to make his undulating way down the field to greet these latest pilgrims.

The parents must sense that he wouldn't hurt a hair on their child's head. He'll take or leave us adults. But for children, there's no end to his patience. Like Ben Beag, he readily accepts their gifts of freshly picked grass, green and rich, that grows beyond his reach.

The children offer it with equal relish, still young enough to be kindred spirits who can imagine how good it tastes.

But there's no horsing around when it comes to their proper feeding.

Perhaps not surprisingly, Big Ben is a stickler for timekeeping. As the hour draws nearer, he or Ben Beag keep watch as people pass over the bridge. I know full well for whom the bell tolls, for as soon as they see me with my buckets, the alarm sounds with a series of neighs.

And though April showers may give him a sore throat, you can be sure Big Ben will never be a little hoarse.

Raising a family of 12 children on a mother's love

'You should write about mothers,' says Paddy Daly, who was head gardener at Mount Juliet back when it was still a 'Big House'. And what better day to do so than this one named in their honour?

Though Paddy wants to talk about 'what the mothers of Ireland suffered, what they went through – because they put up with a lot.'

For while Mary Robinson was 'the nicest woman I met' in all his years in Mount Juliet, the Mna na hEireann of Robinson's presidential victory speech who rocked the system were a less oppressed generation than that of his mother's.

Paddy says it was compulsory to have children in his mother's day.

'If you hadn't had a child in two years, there'd be a knock on the door; it would be a representative from the Legion of Mary or someone like that, wanting to know what was wrong. Increase and multiply; that was the thing. Ridiculous.'

For there was no way to feed all those mouths. Paddy's father, who worked with the hunt in Mount Juliet, used to say that if he left, there'd be 10 lads in the morning looking for his job.

'He was a good father. He never seemed to worry.'

Maybe because that was considered a mother's lot.

'I saw my mother going days without food. Crying in the background and not letting the family know. It was only when she died that I realised what she went through.'

For his mother, he says 'couldn't feed us, couldn't clothe us – 14 people in a house, all on one wage.'

His father dug half an acre to try to help make ends meet.

'The land kept us going; potatoes and cabbage and onions and everything.'

Meanwhile, his mother sold bread that a fellow called Hennessey from Waterford bought. 'She'd make a couple of pence on it. She'd try everything.'

But she was fighting a losing battle. Paddy, who was the second eldest of her 12 children, ended up in a convalescent home in Dublin, suffering from malnutrition. His mother used to write to him. 'She'd put in sweets and every little thing. They couldn't afford to visit me.'

Paddy not only survived but thrived, thanks to his prowess with plants – which was particularly poignant when an operation to give his elderly mother a new lease of life went terribly wrong. It seems symbolic that her heart was so strong that it took a week for her to die.

'I would go in after work every night with a big bunch of flowers, and all the women in the ward would know I was Paddy, the head gardener in Mount Juliet. My mother would be proud as punch and she'd be giving the flowers to all the people.'

One night Paddy went in early to find his mother 'asleep or half asleep, yet she was talking and laughing'. Paddy sat there a long time until she woke up.

'Gosh, Mam, you're in great form,' he said.

'I was talking to Anne,' she told him, referring to his sister who had died when she was 23 years old. Paddy's mother died a few days later. But her son's love for his first lady lives on.

History spans the years to connect all of us

March, with its sunshine but bracing winds, could be seen as the seasonal bridge between winter and summer.

Trees are budding and lambs caper in the fields. Tractors piled high with hay regularly pass over the bridge in this country town.

There is talk of restoring it to the way it was before it was widened for safety reasons some decades ago. Getting rid of the industrial-looking steel railing would certainly help. And surely restoring it shouldn't be seen as a financial bridge too far, considering all the service it has given over the centuries.

So much traffic has passed over it, on foot or horseback, carts or carriages, from bicycles to first bangers and now a steady stream of SUVs.

Lorries still use it, reminding you that old bridges are amazing feats of construction to be able to bear such weight. Indeed, before the motorway was extended here, the traffic over this bridge was heavy-duty and relentless. Some trucks were so massive that other traffic had to wait while they manoeuvred.

Quite impressive, when you consider that many such bridges were built in the time of Scottish folk hero, Rob Roy.

Some bridges are so small that you might not notice them. Many places incorporate bridges in their name, as does our language. Such as 'crossing a bridge when we come to it'.

It was an experience that many Irish people used to dread, says historian Patricia Sharkey, a Derry woman who lives in Donegal. A small stone bridge in the Gaeltacht district of Cloughaneely is known locally as 'Droichead na Caointe' or the 'Bridge of Tears' in English. In the 19th Century, local people emigrating to America and elswhere crossed this bridge on their way to the port of Derry. They were accompanied by family and friends as far as this point, but crossed to the opposite side alone.

I visited the equally unfortunate construct behind the film *The Bridge on the River Kwai* some years ago. A remnant still stands, along with photos of malnourished and malaria-ridden prisioners who died labouring on it.

As I walked over the replica bridge, I realised I was looking at the same view that they once did. How they must have yearned for a glimpse from the bridges of their hometowns.

Nearby is a graveyard for the allied soldiers who died during that war, a vast sea of little white crosses, with the average age engraved on them obscenely young. One that caught my eye was for a Lieutenant Honeybun.

Making me wish as the seasonal stretch in the evening continues, that we always find a bridge over our troubled waters.

Happily, these hogs have been spared the chop

We're almost a fortnight since May Day. But its alternative meaning as an SOS distress signal applied much earlier than that for two sibling swine who were ploughing a local vegetable gardener's field.

Because with two thirds of the land upturned by their equally inclined snouts, time was running out for the soon-to-be-unemployed pair. Their porky prospects were bleak, as they looked doomed to sign off at a slaughterhouse.

I visited the hardworking hogs a few times; a little robin always perched on their enclosure to exploit the ploughed-up easy pickings. The gardener didn't want to get attached, but she delighted in their antics. Such as the way they liked to play at certain times of the day, or loved a scratch with the garden hoe, usually collapsing prostrate with pleasure.

The happy hogs were enjoying a life a million times removed from the gruesome reality that most pigs endure. But I still felt sorry for these two creatures that had been bred to be butchered after a mere six months.

Already ear tags had arrived. And while the gardener gave them no names, they were known as numbers in the bigger picture of pork production. The 'dispatch' papers were ready for a vet to seal their fate by declaring them clean and healthy.

Then I discovered one Friday in April that the gardener had sold them to a man from a country market. He was going to collect them that Sunday and slaughter them the following day.

Yet the field was not fully furrowed. The gardener said the pigs stopped digging within hours of her decision. Instead, they spent most of their time cuddled together as if they sensed what was coming and had given up.

I can't go the whole hog and stop all swinish suffering, but I wanted to save the two that had crossed my path. The gardener agreed to let me find them sanctuary if I covered her costs.

I wasn't optimistic. I only had a weekend. It's heartbreakingly hard enough to home horses or dogs. On top of that, wherever I brought them would have to have a pig herd number.

'Pigs might fly,' I sighed.

But then I struck gold with Deise Animal Sanctuary. Its Noah's ark in Waterford's Nire Valley includes a number of well preserved pigs.

Still, my plea for these trotters was met by momentary silence. But then the English owner, Pat Edwards, spoke three words down the phone line that changed everything.

'All right, darling!'

And so, thankfully, the pigs were.

Punning pubs aren't good enough for the literati

I recently came across an eBook of poetry called *I Love the Internet* by Kevin Barrington, which reminded me of why poetry should be a popular pleasure, rather than the preserve of a finicky few.

It's a lesson I learnt when I first moved to this country town. I'd no fridge, no cooker, and no prospect of either until I sorted out some structural problems.

Worse, it was the tail-end of the Celtic Tiger, when many builders were busy multi-tasking their way to millions constructing 'McMansions' on boggy fields. There were few willing or able to take on my paltry job.

So I had bed, but no breakfast. A town also has its seasons, and while there are evergreen traders here, there were no restaurants open at the time. I didn't know many locals either, though my writerly ways had forged me some literary liaisons. For there are plenty of bohemian types in town.

But I'd as soon watch paint dry as watch dry paint in a frame when I'm hungry, and none of the creative crowd could help me find my way to a hot dinner.

But then something wonderful happened: I discovered the last word in culinary kitsch in a pub called MT Pockets. To my surprise, my high-brow buddies already knew it. But they pooh-poohed its punning name, and the only scoffing they would do was at it, not in it.

Their resistance had no rhyme or reason for me, so I boldly went where no bohemian had gone before, driven by what they considered a lack of taste in my search for something tasty. Which I duly found amid its Seventies' interior, comfy and spacious and replete with wine-coloured velvet couches.

But I saw the appalled look on arty-farty faces when I waxed lyrical about its menu, so I learnt to keep my perverse pleasure to myself.

Until one day a terrible beauty was born. I was sprinkling pepper on my MT Pocket's plate, when in walked a Nobel Prize-winning poet.

He not only looked delighted to be there but to know his way about, confidently leading his party of four down the room.

And so this country town's clever clogs clique discovered that the punning pub was good enough for Ireland's most famous poet, and not just me.

Alas, MT Pockets proved to be poetry in motion, closing its doors soon after. But not before the egghead elite took the poetic licence of changing their tune about it, casually mentioning meals they had enjoyed there as if they'd always done so.

And while I eventually got my kitchen fitted, I still miss those days of 'bard and breakfast'.

Felled family trees bear initials of our ancestors

A young Wexford woman runs the fish van that sets up in my town every Thursday, selling marine miscellany from scallops to salmon.

My Deputy Dawg is her number one fan. Sarah feeds him fishy scraps.

But he got short shrift last week, as the topic of fallen trees preoccupied us. Sarah told me in tragic tones that the oldest tree in the Hook Head Peninsula, on the road to the allegedly haunted Loftus Hall, was felled by a recent storm. It was between 200 and 300 years old.

'All the things it's seen!' she marvelled. 'Wouldn't it be great if we could extract the tree's memory?'

That idea might interest the owner of a nearby estate, who lost up to 30 superb specimens to the storms. She tried to be philosophical, musing that they had to go sometime. Better to be felled by nature's fury than mechanically mown down.

Thankfully, many of her huge, silver-trunked oaks and birches are still standing. Some bear century-old carvings, including the initials of people long since gone. Perhaps their great grandchildren now whizz by them in their cars.

Though many opportunistic drivers were screeching to a halt at the scene of the crime, hopping out with chainsaws in hand to turn fallen trees into free firewood. Some left a sour taste in local mouths by neglecting to tidy up after.

Others slowed down out of self preservation, as trees were viewed as treacherous killers. Then they are as much victims of the vicious weather, their roots left with nothing to grip after months of torrential rain turning the earth to mush, bringing timber titans that stood for aeons to their knotted knees.

It's true that trees can be dangerous, as I discovered on the Dublin to Waterford train during Storm Darwin. We were not far from Kilkenny, when there was an earth shattering sound as a fallen tree literally stopped the train on its tracks. Debris and branches hurtled past the window.

Driver Leo Howard managed to chug us to safety, despite the mudguard being nearly ripped off and the windscreen shattered though intact. A branch was shot through the front of the train, like a Cupid's arrow gone awry.

While we waited for hours for a mini bus, train spotter Frank O'Donoghue from Tramore told me about rugby player William Wesley Twelvetrees. He is nicknamed '36' because of the way Irish fans pronounce his name, which sounds like '12 threes'.

If only that were the total number of wooden wounded, I wouldn't be as gutted as Sarah's van of filleted fish.

Forcing down the facts about motorway meals

One of my favourite anecdotes concerns Mark Twain, who wrote the timeless tales of the adventures of a boy called Tom Sawyer.

While working as a cub reporter, Twain's editor lectured him on only calling something a fact if he was absolutely sure of it. Twain took this advice to heart on his next assignment, which was covering a gala tea party, when he referred to the 'alleged ladies'.

Little has changed – for fact and fiction are still sometimes interchangeable. So feel free to insert inverted commas around words such as 'food' and 'restaurant' in this piece about a dining experience I had en route to this country town.

I was getting petrol at one of those super-sized garages located along motorways that seem to be multiplying in number by the day.

It's been ages since I've ventured inside one to the food hall, but I was hungry – so I decided for old time's sake to order a meal.

The first thing that struck me was the expense. But worse was to come, when this vegetarian lifted the Styrofoam lid and found a rasher sticking out of the bun.

I had barely started explaining the error to the manager, before he tossed the burger in the bin. Since the fries would be cold by the time the correct order arrived, he chucked them too.

The amended meal, when it arrived, was far removed from what I usually put on my plate. Though of course, there was no plate. Or cutlery. All of which made me wonder how I could ever have thought this sort of quick cuisine was cool.

Especially as plastic waste is one of the reasons why this planet is in such a state. Not to mention the impact of these eateries on our physical and psychological health.

There is no time or encouragement for the conveyor belt employees to talk with each other, let alone the customers. Some of whom were growing irate because they had to wait entire minutes for their meals.

Reminding me that the truly appetising options are those country town cafes and restaurants – which these motorway chains are killing off – that are desperate for us to detour to for our meals when on the move. They don't have headquarters in different timezones and are not dictated to by shareholders. And it's hard to imagine them dumping an entire dinner without a thought.

The irony is that these motorway international food chains now lumber along like dinosaurs (or diningsaurs?), and if we're not careful, they will drag us down with them.

No wonder my motorway meal left a bad taste in my mouth.

And a fervent wish that it had been mere fantasy instead of fact.

Of pipe-smoking paddies and kindred spirits

Saint Patrick's Festival may be winding down, but those whose celebrations centred around pubs more than parades are probably still feeling green. At least they'll be spared pinches from any leprechauns still on the lookout for natives not clad in that clichéd colour.

The fact that 'the little folk' inform our festive garb illustrates our unique relationship with otherworldly realms. For instead of fairy tales about magic porridge pots, we share supernatural stories about perpetually smoking pipes.

Ever-bubbling bowls of gruel don't get a mention in this yarn from the Kingdom of Kerry about a tobacco toking ghoul who used to haunt a lonely spot on the road from Dunquin to Ballyferriter. There she would sit on a large rock, terrifying the bejeebers out of passers-by as she puffed away on her pipe.

No wonder most people gave the place a wide berth, taking a roundabout route. Until the night a man doused with Dutch courage after a session with his cronies, and craving a smoke, had the audacity to ask her for a puff.

The surprisingly well-mannered wraith obliged. The chancer took a few puffs, before handing the pipe back with the conventional prayer 'May the Lord have mercy on the souls of your dead!' This he did three times, till the ghost suddenly spoke.

She explained that she was a poor travelling woman who had died there long ago. Her body was never found so no one had uttered a prayer for her repose. But now his prayers had released her from her long vigil.

She gave him the pipe as a parting gift, promising that as long as he kept her tale a secret it would always remain stuffed with tobacco, no matter how much he puffed. Cue one happy chain smoker – talk about coffin nail nirvana!

For so was the case – until the same lubricant that lent him the bravado to cadge off a ghost also caused him to blab. Thus the spell was broken and the old clay pipe was ever more cold and empty.

Much like the heart of the loathsome landlord whose ghost frightened away any folk hoping to find his hidden treasure. All but one servant boy, who volunteered to stay overnight in the haunted house.

He brought with him two bottles that surely encapsulate the concerns of many Irish Catholics. For one contained holy water, while the other was filled with what some call the water of life (known in some quarters as whiskey).

The late lingering landlord clearly agreed, for that night his spiteful spirit crept from the canvas of his portrait, all the while his evil eye fixed on the beckoning bottles. He grabbed one and knocked it back – and vanished with a blue flash and loud crackle, leaving only a smell of brimstone behind.

For this literal demon for the drink chose the wrong bottle and so was evicted into eternity. Leaving the savvy servant to grab his stash of gold that he discovered behind his now empty portrait.

And the rest of us sinners green with envy.

Bridging the gap between heaven and earth

The weather may be a bit of a washout but it looks like we have finally bid a weary farewell to what was a drawn out and dismal winter.

No wonder everyone in this country town is out and about – except for one familiar little figure, that is. For Flying Fauntleroy, the fugitive pigeon, is gone.

I would love to tell you that he flew off into the sunset with a pretty partner with feathers as snowy white as his (though perhaps without the fluorescent band around his leg that was a poignant reminder of his debatably fancy past).

For while no one knows how he ended up living rough around this rural neck of the woods, many believe that he was dumped because he didn't perform well enough, or that his owner would wring his neck if they found him because he failed to come home.

However it happened, this fine fellow with amber eyes that matched the markings on his wings was a living landmark for locals, standing proudly tall on the ramp of the bridge, his puffed out plumage disguising the fact that he was actually famished and begging for food.

Fortunately, while there was no shortage of predictable jokes about pigeon pie, there were plenty of people who obliged this little outsider. From the owner of one cafe who fed him food during last month's snow, when this big white bird was briefly camouflaged; to the diabetic who filled her empty glucose test strip tubes with seed that she carried about in case she saw him; or the not exactly hard-hearted men in the adjacent store.

Though sometimes the paranoid pigeon made a right song and dance before pecking at his food, expending what seemed an awful lot of time and energy on checking that the coast was clear.

Oh, but how right poor little Flying Fauntleroy was. Though he didn't have a chance when death came calling.

For the end was brutal but mercifully swift, according to Catherine, who lives next door to where the pigeon often hung out.

She was in her upstairs kitchen with her granddaughter when 'the next thing there were feathers everywhere. A sparrowhawk swooped down and got him. It was over in seconds'. Though 'you would think the sparrowhawk was a statue, the way he stood on top of him for about two hours before he went off'.

Catherine took a photo through a crack in a metal door; literally like seeing into another world. Which seems appropriate, for while it's sad not to see the familiar little figure on the ramp of the bridge, or flying through the air, so vividly white, before landing on the ugly railings to run awkwardly alongside me in greeting, birds have long been viewed as messengers of the gods and symbols of freedom, who provide us with a bridge between the mundane and spiritual life.

Certainly, this abandoned but brave little bird helped many in this country town to care, and show kindness to another creature. Now he can fly free as a bird in that better world forever.

Sparrowhawks and the savage spice of life

The swallows arrived back last Sunday, three of them soaring over the river in this country town within hours of me wondering when they might return. I felt sad that Flying Fauntleroy, the fugitive pigeon, wasn't here to join them, for a sparrowhawk recently devoured him for dinner.

Yet I was starstruck to find one of these magnificent murderers perched in my back yard the other morning. There stood this musket – as males are called – replete with ferocious stare, fine yellow stockings and stripy vest. He was clearly waiting for me to put out bird food so he could literally grab a bite for breakfast.

It's not my first encounter with Ireland's most common bird of prey. But seeing these chilling, yet charismatic creatures up close, is always thrilling, leading me to despair at folk who berate them because they eat little birds. For they do so to survive, and not for sadistic sport.

Like the pigeon fancier I met who cursed the sparrowhawk that finished off Flying Fauntleroy (you can blame the much bigger femme fatale for that) – he complained there are too many sparrowhawks about.

'Why bring them back?' he raged, referring to the fact that they were once almost wiped out by human destructiveness. 'Once they are gone, leave it at that!'

He even sympathised with farmers who kill them. Though he conceded that intensive agricultural practices of today harm the environment way more than any sparrowhawk ever could.

For while it may be distressing to see songbirds savaged by sparrowhawks, science proves that they do not have a significant detrimental impact on the small bird population.

Far more damaging are domestic cats, which thanks to us occur in much greater numbers than nature can support, wreaking havoc on our native wildlife. Yet the poisoning of birds of prey goes on.

I will never forget the beautiful but lifeless body of a kestrel that I found in Castlefreke, West Cork, some years ago. To destroy such an incredible creature because they threaten our profits, or hamper our hobbies, is surely a sin against all that is sacred.

Thankfully, not everyone wishes them ill.

'There's a breeding pair in the valley at the moment,' enthuses a local. 'You see them around twilight each evening. It's fantastic that sparrowhawks are back in the area. It's nature at its best.'

These particular birds of prey live up to their name, as an anecdote about the aged Duke of Wellington illustrates.

The Duke was summoned by Queen Victoria for advice on how to clear an infestation of hundreds of sparrows from the glass roof of Crystal Palace. All attempts had failed; it was too high for nets and no guns could be used as even the sound of blanks might shatter the glass.

The Duke just drawled: 'Sparrowhawks, Ma'am.'

Sure enough, two of them cleared the sparrows in minutes.

If I didn't know better, I'd find that hard to swallow.

Tranquillity is all too often the road less taken

I was thinking of moving to the country and had peeked at a few places, before I came across this particular town cottage.

Nothing special from the outside, but cosy within – it was only when I saw the river out back that I was sold. This force of nature that is the width of a modern road was the deal-maker for me.

Unlike the deal-breaker, which hundreds of worried residents consider the N6 Galway City Transport Project to be. They are protesting against the six proposed routes, which they believe will split local communities in half and cause mayhem.

The whole mess caused by building a motorway so close to the Hill of Tara illustrates that some spaces should be considered sacred. Arguably, that also includes secular ones.

As Mike Geraghy of the N6 Action Group says: 'you're talking about people's homes'. Which is where the heart is – so surely that should count for something in the scheme of things?

More worrying, they also say that you don't know what you've got 'til it's gone. Which is especially true of precious, yet imperceptible paraphernalia – such as atmosphere, intimacy and character. As the sales signs in shops remind us: once it's gone, it's really gone.

Only then, you might notice the difference. Like the time I was in a remote part of Donegal, on a hill overlooking a modern road that had been imposed on an area of natural – and, indeed, supernatural – significance, being rich in folklore. I was struck by the sense that something pristine had been ripped out by the road running through the place.

Small-scale sacrilege often takes place on our doorsteps. Some of the history of this country town was destroyed decades ago, when all the houses on one side of the road where I live in Thomastown were demolished and replaced by a car park.

Likewise, the road, off which a vet I sometimes attend is located, was recently widened, to become efficient but anonymous.

'They killed it,' as Olive, the receptionist put it. 'That lovely country road is gone forever.'

Old roads are sometimes wickedly winding – because they went around things, rather than bulldozing their way through. Modern ones have no such manners, as the plight of a poignant old house outside the nearby city exemplifies.

Talk about being in the wrong place at what is now the wrong time. It is marooned in less-than-splendid isolation, thanks to a mammoth ring road and a series of roundabouts. This once impressive property is stranded like a shipwreck from a forsaken century.

Galway residents fear a similar fate. It seems we care more about parking cars than about communication and quality of life.

But prioritising 'going' over 'being' is something we might regret down the road.

A time of fond farewells and comfy coffins

It was a beautiful May morning when I met a man in this country town whose wife had recently passed away. Though he blinked back tears, he said that he had no regrets. For he had honoured the vows made when his beloved was terminally ill, and truly loved her in both sickness and health.

As her primary carer, he had attended to her needs day-in, day-out for over a decade, never complaining about a cross he willingly bore because of love.

It meant his wife enjoyed the all-too-rare privilege nowadays of having control over medication to alleviate her pain. (This may have included several stiff gin and tonics and cigarettes.)

Standing in the sunshine, her widower looked worn out, yet radiant. He spoke fondly about the funeral, which had been simplicity itself, a civil ceremony that celebrated his beloved's life.

Such an informal farewell is still not the norm. Yet in many ways, the attitude was similar in the 1940s, for people were less daunted by death. Like WH Auden's poem *Funeral Blues* (which was famously recited in the film *Four Weddings and a Funeral*) the custom then was to stop the clocks and leave the dearly departed alone for a while, to allow them time for a quiet word with God.

Indeed, some folk were so fine with their fate that they kept a coffin in the house in case they died unexpectedly. As an old lady remembers: 'T'was nice to have a coffin handy in case you wanted the auld box at short notice.'

Though a story recounted by John Fitzgerald in his book about that era, *Are We Invaded Yet?* suggests that some people were far too comfy around coffins long before their time.

Like the man who developed the habit of dropping into the funeral house at the end of a long night of liquid refreshments. If an open coffin happened to be lying about, he would climb in and doze off, making himself scarce before the undertakers arrived.

All was well with his free board on funeral boards, until he overslept one morning. The earthly administrator for the angel of death found him curled up in the coffin, snoring heavily enough to wake the dead. He decided to play a prank on this imposter. Wrapping himself in a white sheet, he stood over the coffin.

'Arise!' he called out. 'Arise – it's the last day.'

The befuddled boozer opened his eyes to find a white shrouded figure hovering over him in the dimmed room.

'God, what's happening?' he shrieked, 'Where am I?'

'Yer in trouble,' replied the would-be grim reaper. 'Yer late for the feckin' resurrection! I'm taking you off now. Get up and we'll be going – the hearse is outside. Ah, heaven is a lovely place.'

Clearly the man wasn't quite ready to swap a nap for full-blown nirvana. He jumped from the coffin and ran away from the building. They say he never touched a drop of the hard stuff again.

Unlike the many who toasted his teetotalling transformation at his eventual wake.

When fish on a Friday was fine — but not fishing

Many in this country town will eat fish on Good Friday – though whether they fancy a bit of battered cod and chips, rather than deference to religious dogma is debatable. Yet even when Lent was almost law, plenty had heathen hearts. Which emigration exacerbated by exposing them to godless ways.

Or so seems to be the case in a tale from Eddie Lenihan's collection *The Devil Is An Irishman*, about the conflict between superstitious spirituality and progressive pragmatism experienced by an emerging modern Ireland.

It is set in a tightly-knit community in Galway during the 1920s, where folk make their living from the sea. Except on Fridays. 'That's the day Our Saviour suffered for us... it wasn't worked in our father's time, and it won't be worked in ours either.'

As Lenihan wryly notes, 'outsiders shrugged at these quaint notions, those merchants with contracts to fill fretted, and even the local priests were prepared to intervene and negotiate a dispensation. But the ancients of the Claddagh were immovable'.

Until Sean O'Duinnin – 'the pride of the village' – hungers for adventure and heads to the British 'Big Smoke' where he heeds his mother's advice to 'mind your religion...' even if he went no further than the church door and could hardly see the priest, let alone hear him.

He thrives, thanks to hard work and 'his native Galway gobbiness'. Plus he never drinks 'to stupefaction like other lonely Irish bachelors'.

Years slip by, until one day Sean seeks shelter during a sudden downpour in Highgate Cemetery. He is horrified when lightning illuminates a grave bearing his name, especially 'in an English – worse, a London – graveyard!' It's enough to make Sean finally head home, where his savings buy a big boat that employs everyone.

Which means happy days – though Sean bullies them into working on the supposedly sacred one of Friday.

But the community adjusts, until 'the matter of Friday fishing as a topic of conversation, even of casual reference, was by now long a thing of the past; people no longer even questioned why they had ever held such a foolish, nonsensical belief'.

But there are limits, for the crew refuse to fish on Good Friday. Sean is furious and jumps at the offer of a sinister stranger to do the entire crew's work. Sean is delighted when he nets the biggest catch of his life.

Until he discovers the even bigger catch is his life. For the stranger is the devil – and Sean's soul is his wages.

Thankfully, the crucifix that Sean's long-suffering mother gave him scares off Satan. And while there is sympathy when Sean loses his boat, 'most felt that right had triumphed'.

And so 'there was no more Friday fishing... the clergy read it most thoroughly from the altar as the devil's own work. And for once they had the complete support of the people'.

Though perhaps a few pagans – peeved at losing the freedom to work on Friday – took the devil's side and privately pointed the fish finger.

May is the month to remember the many Marys

'May is the month of Mary' – though this one is also when the 'Repeal the Eighth' Referendum takes place, as placards around this country town remind us. Apparently, abortion happened in ancient Ireland, but a woman who found herself with an unwanted pregnancy 100 years ago most likely ended up in a County Home.

These were the last refuges for the powerless in Irish society. 'There'd be old people who had no home and were in bad health,' says local Paddy. 'Ten or 20 of them could die in a week if they got the flu.'

And if life was cheap for these unfortunate citizens, then death was even more undignified. For they were buried in 'the shank yard', as locals called the field behind the Home.

'They'd bring them up there with a horse and cart; no priest, no prayers, no nothing. Dig a trench and tip them in – they kept filling it in the whole time. People arriving afterwards, from America, looking for their relatives were distressed because they couldn't find them.'

Paddy knows all this, not just because he's 'always been big into history'. For his grandmother was born in the County Home. 'I did the family history and found her birth cert and sponsors.'

His mother rarely mentioned her.

'But she knew. We were once at a wedding in a fancy venue and she said: 'look at this place, this should have been mine.'

For 'the culprit' was from a wealthy background. 'But he fecked off to America and left her there. The men who did it got away with it and it was covered up. Being illegitimate, my mother had no say. And being a woman, she had less than that.'

Paddy remembers the old uncle who 'would have a bit of pity on my mother and gave her some money at Confirmations and birthdays. She'd shove it down into her pocket.'

Many girls who 'got into trouble', worked as domestics, like the young Church of Ireland servant from Carlow that Paddy's mother remembered. 'She got pregnant by the butler and her parents wouldn't take her back.'

The girl drowned in the river.

'The women in the big house laid her out in a dress. They took her in a cart with two lanterns to the graveyard at night, so no one would see.'

Paddy's great grandmother, Mary, was also a servant. 'When the time came, she was put into the County Home to have the child.'

Mary left her there and later married. But tragedy wasn't done with her, for Mary and her family all perished in a fire.

What happened to the baby girl, who would become Paddy's grandmother, is in some ways just as perturbing. A local family took her out of the house and reared her. 'They treated her well.'

When she came of age, one of them married her. 'That happened a lot. It was either that, or stay in the County Home till she was 16. They were taken into homes, used for scrubbing floors.'

All because they were guilty of being born to an unmarried Mary.

Rebellion is in our blood, not just in the water

April was doubly uplifting thanks to a spell of sizzling weather over the holidays that celebrated the Christian resurrection.

But while Irish Easter Risings extend beyond prayerful piety into political proclamations, it seems what goes up must come down. For today, like many other May days, is the anniversary of executions of the 1916 leaders.

People here are still protesting, from pensioners to pro-lifers. Rural Ireland wants pylons and wind farms to lay off the land, while urbanites argue over inequalities in the property tax. Now water charges have come to the fore, a housing estate in the rebel county recently obstructing the installation of meters *(April 2014)*.

You could dub these dissenters 'Waterboys'. But perhaps the powers that be should worry about them morphing into Whiteboys.

That was the name of gangs in 18th-century Ireland who spread terror to protest against unfair taxes, whether from government, landowners or the Church of Ireland.

However, it wasn't just persecuted tenants rising against cruel landlords. Sometimes it was labourer against labourer, forming mobs to deny work to men from other districts, or even men from their own district, whose claim, they held, was not as great as their own.

The Whiteboys sometimes wore a disguise of a white shirt over a woman's skirt, their heads covered by a cowl and straw, or faces blackened with soot. The white shirts became a symbol of violence and gave them their most popular name, but they were also known as Steelboys, Levellers, Oakboys, Rockites or Molly Maguires.

Their aspect was said to be so terrifying that often it needed only their appearance outside a man's house to have him instantly yield to their demands – whether to leave his farm, refuse to pay rent and so risk eviction, or dismiss one employee and hire another.

The phenomenon purportedly began in 1760 in Kilmallock, Co. Limerick, when a lawyer and gentleman farmer called William Fant decided upon a unique way to settle his grievances against the landed gentry.

He gathered a large crowd around him on a market day in the town and made a violent speech, alleging that certain lands were commons illegally enclosed. He then led the crowd to demolish the fences.

The idea became popular and spread to other parts of Munster and beyond. From levelling fences they went on to maiming cattle, burning hay, trampling crops, and attacking people, burning houses and killing men, women and children.

Let's hope leaking water pipes don't turn into ticking bombs.

SUMMER

The loudness of the lambs — and Julie Lambert

Lambs are frolicking in summer fields sprinkled with bright yellow buttercups. The sun was setting as I passed a flock of the fleecy fellows recently, when they decided to enjoy one more caper on the cusp of dusk. They charged up field, before coming to an abrupt halt and then bounding in the opposite direction.

Maybe they were making the most of it: playfully prancing before they end up on a plate.

One dinner they won't be gracing is that of a local shopkeeper. This country-town version of the movie character Clarice Starling never eats lamb, because she grew up next door to where they were silenced.

Regardless of culinary choices, many people have a soft spot for these soft-coated cuties.

For most, having a pet lamb remains the monopoly of a nursery rhyme Mary. Which, incidentally, was the first piece the evidently envious inventor Thomas Edison recorded over a hundred years ago.

But the aptly named Julie Lambert got lucky. Because forget Skippy the kangaroo – this fifty-something once had Skippy the much-loved pet lamb.

'We were always hoping for one,' says Julie, who grew up on a farm. 'But daddy said we couldn't, though we begged him.'

Then one time something happened to a sheep. Her lamb was very sick, so Julie and her sister brought him inside. They nursed him at the fire and fed him warm milk. Afterwards they made him a bed in an old car in the field, filling it with straw.

Julie remembers running across the ditch to him the morning after. 'My sister said, "I bet he's dead." I said, "I bet he's alive." And there he was, standing looking out the car window at us!'

That was it; they kept Skippy and fed him.

'He became so attached to us. He thought he was one of the family.'

So much so that Skippy used to come upstairs to go to the toilet. 'Mammy would be running after him with the brush. We were afraid she'd catch him but he was really fast, because he was a ram lamb.'

Julie and her sister used to walk three miles to their national school.

'We'd be coming home and about a mile away, we'd start shouting "Skippy!" And he'd come flying out to meet us!'

But the good times didn't last.

'Skippy started eating mammy's flowers when he got older. We said, "Sure, so what? It's only flowers." But mammy said he'd have to go out to the field with the sheep.'

There, a sad Skippy sat pining at the gate.

'We used to hear him roaring. We knew he was missing us, and we were missing him. After that, I said I couldn't go down the road of having a pet lamb. The heartbreak was too much.'

Easy to believe, so I couldn't say baa humbug to that.

A facelift alone won't make a town shine

This country town has nifty new street furniture – thanks to the powers-that-be finally starting to provide support via renewal schemes for rural communities.

But once the diggers are done, will the town itself collude to undo the good work?

Take the pristine and widened pavements. Will those dog owners who think the rest of us enjoy picking up after our pets treat them as extra large toilets for Toto?

And some children need to be reminded to use those brand new bins for ridding themselves of their rubbish – not the river and its surrounds. Otherwise, scenic spots that draw in tourists and passing trade will become eyesores.

Because, while outside intervention is imperative, the choices a community itself makes also determines whether a town survives and thrives, or continues its downward spiral into becoming a dive full of boarded-up buildings.

For every time we buy online or at international supermarkets – though we know local shops sell similar goods – we play our part in pulling down our town.

As it is, many small businesses are only hanging in because of sheer bloody-mindedness. A clothes shop on this town's main street that has managed to stay open for over 150 years reminds me of a pioneering outpost from the Wild West whenever I step through its doors, thanks to the air of energy and cheerfully adapting.

Much of it comes from the proprietor, who is full of beans and sassy with it. How else to explain a sign on one wall that reads: 'Grow your own dope – plant a man?' It always has an imaginative window display, even though business has taken a battering over the past decades. But it has diversified into being a barber, as well as providing an outlet for another local's alteration business.

The health store a few doors up, though a toddler in comparison, recently celebrated 10 years of trade – no mean feat. But who knows how much longer it can survive, without the means to offer the loyalty cards and special offers that international chains can afford.

Meanwhile, several bookies in town continue to prosper. People also queue to do the Lotto, some regularly spending a small fortune in the hope of hooking the big financial fish. Everyone is looking for a quick fix, to skip the struggle and go straight to the prize.

Yet the real risk-takers that we need to back are local businesses – for their gamble is grounded in reality and hard graft.

And since every open shop adds spirit and sparkle to a small town's streets, shouldn't the wider community share the high stakes by offering support?

For we need to put our money where our mouth is – and our neighbours and children need to, also.

Because fabulous new fittings alone won't copperfasten their future.

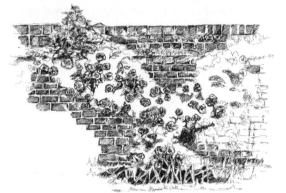

Summer is shifting, like the sands of time

This new month finds the countryside still in full bloom, with the fields and virgin forests surrounding this country town proving the '40 shades of green' claim not only true but, indeed, maybe underestimating the number. The resemblance of some pastoral parts to tropical rainforests owes much to the humidity, sudden rain showers and all too short splashes of sunshine of this summer's somewhat mixed bag.

But less than lovely or not, the arrival of August means that summer is simmering down and autumn is fast approaching. As the blonde bombshell butcher reminded me when I was buying Deputy Dawg's dinner recently, and she remarked that the evenings were beginning to draw in.

I admit that I hadn't noticed, but plenty of other locals agreed with her less than optimistic observation. Proving that even if it's too nippy for a seaside dip, we can still put our head in the rain-sodden sand when it comes to seeing only what we want to see.

For open your eyes and you quickly realise that the signs of shifting seasons are everywhere. Apples are budding on 100-year-old trees up the hill, and the horse chestnuts are well on their way to producing shiny brown conkers.

While a glance at the window display of uniforms in Woods on Main Street confirms that both the new school year and the darkening cold are creeping closer.

So best take your cue from the feverish farmers whose tractors trundle back and forth over the bridge from dawn to dusk these days, and make hay while the sun shines. Though not by rolling up your sleeves to get stuck into another important project, but by rolling down your car window or indeed pulling over altogether to smell those roses that are in ridiculous abundance wherever you go, spilling over the fences and crumbling stone walls of country cottages to carpet the grass beneath with cerise-pink petals.

Because not only will this summer swiftly pass, but as those studies of the dying poignantly point out, who knows how many we have left? Yet most of us tend to live as if, like those 40 shades of green, we have an infinite number to savour.

For all too often, it's only when we lose someone – or else our health – that the wistful words of those soon to be departed remind us of the regrets that we might one day harbour.

They express the same sentiments over and over again: how they wish they had stayed in touch with friends. Or lived the life they wanted, rather than the one they felt was expected of them.

And nowadays, it's not only men who regret having worked too hard.

Above all, they mourn the lack of courage to have let themselves be happier.

So make August a wickedly wonderful month. And you'll live wisely – whatever the weather.

Why happy communities are out to lunch

Life seems light-hearted in this wonderful weather, what with June 'bustin' out all over' as *Carousel* proclaims. Trees resemble giant broccoli again, while hedgerows are a shock of green and white, thanks to cow parsley. Wild cherry trees have replaced last month's haunting blasts of hawthorn, with crab apple in bloom adding a romantic pink blush.

No wonder laughter is also easy, as illustrated by the blackboard I spotted recently outside a pub in a nearby village.

'Hungry?' it reads. 'We have food. Thirsty? We have alcohol. Lonely? We have Fintan.'

Social isolation is hard to imagine when the sun is shining, yet its darkness persists beneath the lengthening days, with untold numbers of troubled souls among us. And unlike those immortalised in Ralph McTell's *Streets of London* – one of the most recorded songs ever, significantly – they are not confined to cities.

This is the case in Ireland, thanks to a health system that leaves many who are mentally ill drifting through towns and villages, where they linger a while before disappearing to heaven knows where.

Those passing through this country town come in all sad shapes and sizes, of both genders, young and older. Rarely are they obvious at first sight. It is only when you see them still hunched by the river, long after the sun has set and other folk have gone home or to meet friends, that you realise something is amiss.

It isn't just strangers who suffer in silence. There are neighbours and acquaintances who appear cheerful; a façade that fades once they close their front doors behind them.

Even this tight-knit community has not escaped the suicide epidemic that continues to plague our country.

There have been a few awful occasions since I moved here when I've woken up to find tables set up on the far riverbank.

Alas, these are not bearing refreshments for a kayaking competition or a TidyTowns clean-up; they are there to provide sustenance for volunteers searching for locals who have gone ominously missing.

What's more, despite all the media hype about folk feeling happier as they age, increasingly it is older people who are struggling most. The closure of traditional centres of social interaction – the pub, post office and small, community-based businesses – undoubtedly plays a pivotal part in their sense of abandonment and irrelevance.

All the more reason then, to celebrate today's seventh annual Street Feast, the brainchild of a group of volunteers who wanted to find a way to reduce isolation and boost community resilience. These life-affirming lunches hosted by locals for locals are taking place across the country.

When life piles too much on your plate, isn't it better to share?

Timely tale of the white-haired boy and a debt repaid

Some say our nearest neighbour has sent itself to Coventry by bidding adieu to the EU. But this tale that spans an Irish town and the English one of that very name, seems reassuring about our unique relationship.

Steve was a labourer's son of about 10 when the British paramilitary troops known as the 'Black and Tans' (20% of whom were actually Irish or of Irish descent) were 'raging through the Irish countryside'.

According to awesome octogenarian Ned Egan, 'they were genuine hard men from the trenches and battles of Verdun and Picardy. Where, according to the sweet old song, "roses were blooming" – on the graves of young men, their former comrades, mostly.'

But the Tans liked Steve and gave 'the little blond tearaway' the run of the barracks. Which 'the chirpy little gorsoon found most profitable. But as the stuff he filched was always HM's and not personal, they didn't give a shite.'

Then one day, Steve discovered a badly-injured man in a torn Tan uniform chained up in a truck in the barracks. He begged for water and Steve obliged.

The man explained that he got a letter saying his girl had dumped him. So he stole a Lee Enfield rifle and sold it 'to one of your lads' – the IRA – so he could go drinking.

The doomed man was to be executed as a traitor the following morning. 'But I've killed enough people now for the King, and I'm sick of it all,' he said. 'I'll be glad to go.' Adding 'thanks forever' to Steve for his kindness.

'You look like the little brother I used to have – he was blond as well. We called him the White-Haired Boy. He died at Verdun, but sometimes he visits me in dreams.'

Years later – like many a Paddy – Steve went to England to work in the town of Coventry. When World War II started, Steve and his elderly landlady, Lizzie, used to camp in her cellar when the sirens went.

One night, a bomb whammed through the house and buried itself in a corner of the cellar. But – incredibly – it didn't go off.

Finally, the Air Raid Precaution Warden thought the bombing was finished, but that they should stay there until the all clear.

'By the way,' he added, 'anyone down there named the White-Haired Boy? A strange geezer up the street wants to see him. Said it's urgent, and to bring his friend. I wouldn't bother if I were you.'

But Steve immediately got his landlady out of the cellar. The warden called them 'bloody daft buggers'. But he pointed down the street and Steve corralled his landlady there.

'Well, Steve,' said Lizzie, 'I just don't know what all that ruddy fuss was ab…' – and then the whole area shook 'like an earthquake had decided to join the war!'

A minute later, her house was 'only a smoking hole in the ground'. It turned out the bomb had been a delayed action device.

As Ned put it: 'From a great distance – from another time – a debt had been repaid.'

For life – like leaving the EU – is rarely black and white.

Finding common ground
between city and country

Cities are often cited as Meccas of multiculturalism that are down with diversity. But it takes more than a love of skinny lattes to be truly liberal, especially if your core is conservative.

So if you want to experience egalitarianism, come to a country town.

The saying 'it takes all sorts' really comes to life in any rural community worth its salt. Like the farmer who enjoys shooting the breeze with this vegetarian, unfazed by how vile I consider the treatment of 'livestock', as such folk euphemistically refer to those sentient beings that are bred to be butchered.

In true country fashion, we've helped each other out over the years; this friendly farmer offering me lifts when thieves temporarily relieved me of my motor, while I contacted him when his cattle broke free from their field.

Sometimes he'll mention an old country custom or superstition, before worrying that I'll broadcast it countrywide via this column.

The truth is that he's one of my favourite people around these parts. Maybe because beneath the butchery and unabashed love of steak, I suspect he has a kind heart.

Certainly, he's smart enough to have pulled off a bit of provincial paradise for himself, being father to five fine children and with a fair and lovely lady for his wife.

Of course, being Irish means he's also a charming mass of complexity and contradiction. He's fond of casually quoting Shakespeare in the sauna – where many around here gather for steamy sessions – after a day spent sweating over pregnant ewes.

While, like many of us, he is suspicious of change, believing it rarely is for the better. Yet he embraces blow-ins, such as this former city slicker, being of the view that they bring fresh blood and stimulus to the country life table.

Maybe it isn't so funny that we get on. After all, we have in common finding each other's attitude to animals a bit absurd.

But while we are miles apart when it comes to meat, we share a love of nature – as well as a general nosiness.

Take the time I was having a closer look at his lambs, when he arrived with one of his sons and loaded them in a trailer. I asked their fate, wondering if he was sending them to slaughter, and in response he beckoned me to his battered Jeep.

Next thing I knew, I was sitting in the back next to his son as he drove us to heaven knows where.

We passed the turn that farmers often take when livestock are doomed to become late stock. We wound down country lanes, his son and I chatting about all and sundry, from his favourite subjects in school to the fact that I don't eat animals.

Mr Farmer watched from the rear-view mirror as I explained my views to his interested offspring, looking as happy as Larry.

Finally we arrived at his farm, where he unloaded the lambs before dropping me home.

But while we live and let live, forgive me for hoping that one day he'll extend the same courtesy to his cattle.

Time to abandon noxious chemical war on weeds

White signs are dotted along the riverbank in this country town this summer. 'Managed for wildlife' they read, above a drawing of a bumblebee getting stuck into a pink-headed thistle.

It's a welcome antidote to the scary looking outfits, like something out of science fiction, worn by folk spraying weedkiller outside supermarkets, schools and along country roads.

Such pesticides keep golf courses as pristine and lifeless as the lawns of the McMansions that seem to be sprouting up everywhere, turning once fertile fields and magical meadows into sad still-lifes of suburban sameness – bereft of birds and bees.

I can't remember the last time I saw a ladybird.

For the war we have long waged on weeds adversely affects insects and wildlife. As Rachel Carson's groundbreaking book, *Silent Spring*, published in 1962, put it, the 'mindset that advocated chemicals as weapons on farms, pastures and forests set the course of war in Vietnam. Chemicals – herbicides contaminated with dioxin as well as napalm – were our weapons of mass destruction'.

Indeed, two days before her book came out, President Kennedy signed his approval for the so-called 'rainbow herbicides' (Agents Orange, White,

Purple, Green, Pink and Blue, named for the coloured bands on the herbicide barrels) to be sprayed on Vietnamese crops.

Operation Ranch Hand increased significantly under Lyndon Johnson – the intensive environmental abuse giving rise to the term 'ecocide'.

As Carson anticipated, the powerful agrichemical industry went on the attack even before her book was published. Nevertheless, *Silent Spring* resulted in sweeping environmental change.

The US herbicide programme ended in 1971, when Nixon's administration was forced to disclose covered-up research data about one of the herbicides in Agent Orange.

Not before 40% of coastal mangrove forests, inestimable marine nurseries, and more than five million acres of upland forests and agricultural lands were destroyed.

Is it a chilling coincidence that one of the biggest producers of Agent Orange – Monsanto Chemical Co – produces Roundup, the most popular weedkiller in the world today?

Many farmers who rely on Roundup to control weeds are furious that it may soon be banned in the EU because of fears surrounding a key ingredient – glyphosate – which in 2015 the World Health Organisation's cancer agency said it believed it 'probably' caused cancer in humans.

This was disputed last year by a committee known as the RAC, which agreed to restrict warnings to the current advice that Roundup can cause 'serious eye damage' and is 'toxic to aquatic life with long-lasting effects'.

Leaving me wondering why those riverbank signs are painted white, the symbolic colour of surrender.

And how easy the living really is for the fish jumping beneath them this summertime.

It's not just the fair sex who suffered unfairly

Some 'Repeal the Eighth' supporters viewed the referendum as the latest struggle in a long history of female oppression in this country. But in some ways injustice was ironically more equal in the not so good old days.

For while the wretched treatment of women has been brought to light, there is much less mention of the brutality inflicted on the poor boys and men who had the misfortune to also be incarcerated in Ireland's County Homes.

'I remember going to school with some of the boys, and they used to wear what was known as County Home shirts; no necks on them and real rough,' says Noel, a local in his 80s. 'And a big old pair of boots.'

His great friendship with one of the boys, Tommy Webster, was savagely cut short when Tommy was 14, for that was when the County Home would give the boys out to the farmers 'for nothing. Some did all right but others were little more than slaves. They'd be up in the loft, with no room or bed, sleeping in the hay.'

For most farm labourers were men from County Homes, 'men who had nothing. Sometimes they would come into town and have a drink and back a few horses. But then they got rowdy and would be locked up in a sort of cell. They'd get a fair few clatters and other abuse before they were let out again in the morning.'

This was going on long before Noel was born.

'When my father was young, he told me about the time he called to a farm, where he heard there was a vacancy for work. He was waiting in the yard and saw a man over 70 years of age working in the hayloft. He was slowing down – he was all pains and everywhere – but the owner of the farm roared up to him: "If you don't get that done in 10 minutes, I'll put you in the County Home!"

My father got on his bike and went straight home again.'

But there was no escape for those without means, especially from the master who ran the County Home.

'He had total power over everything – including access to the young girls. He signed for all the provisions and did all the buying in of the food. The cheaper he could get it, the more he would have for himself.'

And the master did a mercilessly good job of ensuring he made a tidy profit.

'They had a cauldron and put a beef head in it. It was only coloured water. That would do 100 people.'

It sounds farcical, though it must have been tragic for those famished souls who depended on it, but the Home had to go through a Board of Guardians, made up of big farmers and other pillars of society, to get permission to put in a few carrots or parsnips.

'Imagine a beef head in the cauldron,' Noel shakes his head, 'and having to apply to the authorities to add an onion.'

They got two slices of bread and a bit of butter to go with a bowl of that broth.

'And skimmed milk – they wouldn't get the cream. That was the staple diet of those old farm labourers.'

Making them victims, as much as those unfortunate members of the fair sex, of a most unfair era.

Life's a dirty beach, because of litter louts

A friend in need is a friend indeed – and this heatwave makes me very glad that I am living in a coastal country.

They invite me to visit, so I knock off work early and break for the border. The seaside looks stunning from the cliff top, but the ugly underbelly blighting all this beauty soon becomes evident. For some absolute, and literal, tossers are turning our beaches toxic with their litter.

I've cooled down from a swim, but within minutes I'm boiling mad – for cans, plastic and cartons are scattered everywhere on the sand. And glass bottles are falling from the rocks behind us, the draining of the alcohol attracting a swarm of flies.

Only a minority toss their litter away. But that's enough to ruin the experience for everybody, and more importantly, it devastates the environment. Those little fish swimming around my toes will soon have this crap swirling around them.

I start picking up bottles; furious because it's roasting hot and my time off is precious. Soon my bag is full, yet I've barely scratched the surface of one small area.

Then I notice an attractive woman who has arrived on the beach. It's after 8pm and temperatures are still soaring. But instead of carrying a picnic basket, she's dragging a black refuse bag behind her.

She throws her dogs a stick – and bends down to pick up someone else's rubbish.

'This is a beautiful beach, so I'm trying to keep it that way,' she replies, when I ask her what she's doing. 'I pick up the rubbish because somebody has to. Have you seen that footage of the sea horses clutching a Q-tip?'

The litter comes 'mainly from younger people – you can tell by the kind of rubbish left behind…soft-drink bottles, beer bottles, cans of drink.'

Litter has its own foul seasons, with the Irish summer tourists dumping 'beer cans, nappies, underwear'.

Meanwhile, in winter months, it's usually plastic that gets washed up.

'Most people are gone when we come down every evening and you see what's left behind. You expect to see the sea sparkling – not beer cans.'

Her 'we' refers to just herself and her daughters. To add to our shame, she's not Irish. This woman, from Wales, has been living in rural Ireland for 27 years.

What would solve Ireland's crappy crisis that sees beaches abused and tides turned into toilets?

'Bins would help!' she laughs. 'And emptying them regularly. Plus plenty of signage, with "leave nothing but footprints behind" written on them, and the like.'

We could all do with adjusting our behaviour, and she admits 'the nappies really annoy me – because that's young mothers. If that's what your children see you doing, then what hope is there?'

The family behind us are getting ready to leave and checking they haven't forgotten anything. But others have forgotten their responsibility to raise environmentally aware children.

Dumping the dire consequences on the rest of us.

Our beauty spots are becoming building sites

A town is a living thing, so naturally this one has changed since I moved here a decade ago, shutters coming down on shops and bank branches, and the post office pushed to its perimeters. Thankfully, there are bright new lights, along with die-hards that hang in despite everything.

But what is not so great is this town stretching its tentacles beyond traditional borders to build an oversized suburbia. As a woman who was away working in Australia discovered when a neighbour phoned.

'You know those wildflower fields behind your cottage?' she said. 'Well, they're gone.' Replaced by one of several housing estates tacked on over the last couple of decades.

Our British buddies across the water have a massive population compared to us, yet they still protect and preserve their countryside and towns.

Whereas anyone who owns land here seems more or less free to sell it off for a pretty penny. Even though the entire town pays the price for their personal profit, not to mention the considerable ecological consequences.

And it is getting worse. The expanding dairy industry has forced many beef farmers out of business, benefiting builders and developers after a quick buck. An estate agent placard has been peeping from the hedgerows half a mile outside this town for ages, advertising dozens of sites for sale, all resulting in rural Ireland being razed to the ground to be replaced with plots for concrete monstrosities.

A drive up any country road is an exercise in dismay as you glance towards the gap, expecting a meadow, only to be met by another ugly McMansion.

I wonder if their residents ever reflect on how their huge new homes were recently the habitat of local wildlife. Or does money always matter more than the survival of other mammals? Are creatures without credit cards viewed as trespassing vermin, pests to shoot, snare or poison?

Judging by those lifeless lawns, I'm not optimistic.

Because it would be one thing if they built something in scale with the surroundings, as humans did back when we had a little humility about our place in the grand scheme of things.

For hubris surely lies behind the houses getting bigger as families grow smaller – and the trend of buying a site with a ruin, known as a footprint, that allows them to plant a bully boot nearby.

For usually the old homestead is overshadowed by a cement colossus, as if contemptuous of the countryside and existing period dwellings.

Massive new builds on one-acre plots are now often the first thing you see when you enter Irish villages and towns. So why do we delude ourselves that building on a beauty spot is democracy instead of destruction, ironically, of what belongs to all of us?

Isn't it time we demanded strict standards for dwellings, or developments that we lay on our precious land?

And show our love for it by not allowing greed and financial gain for a few to flatten our green fields forever.

Driven to despair and destroyed by dreams of gold

This little island has a long history of emigration. Many a family in this country town have at least one child living abroad, whether just across the water or further afield.

Such is the case with my late brother's friend, Finbarr, who lives in the major port city of Fremantle in Western Australia.

He tells me that if you wander down the beach to watch the sunset, you will also see a bronze statue of a man on horseback in the ocean, looking back over his shoulder at Fremantle Harbour.

You might assume this mythical sight is connected to the Aboriginals, who have the longest continuous cultural history of any group of people on Earth. Their Creation Myth teaches that ancestor spirits made the world, before changing into trees, the stars, rocks, watering holes and so on – making nature, and not man-made objects, sacred.

Yet that statue of a man on horseback almost submerged in the sea is actually an Irishman. Charles Yelverton O'Connor found fame and glory as an engineer in Western Australia during the succession of gold rushes that caused a population explosion in its barren and dry desert centre.

Fremantle Harbour was probably O'Connor's greatest triumph, as his proposal to build it within the entrance to the Swan River was regarded as almost impossible.

But his work on the Goldfields Water Supply Scheme – perhaps the world's longest water main – was his downfall.

For a vicious campaign, motivated by political agendas and individual greed, plagued O'Connor towards the end of the project. A typically libellous article in the *Sunday Times* in 1902 accused 'this crocodile imposter' of corruption.

Mental illness caused by overwork and worry, along with many health problems – including cirrhosis of the liver – meant O'Connor never got to see his engineering wonder at work when it was completed in 1903.

Because on March 10, 1902, O'Connor mounted his favourite horse and rode out into the Indian Ocean – where he shot dead both horse and himself.

The statue stands on the spot he committed suicide.

But they say that the real cause of O'Connor's demise was a curse placed on him by local Aboriginals for destroying their environment. Specifically, by blasting away the limestone bar across that part of the Swan River, which was a source of food for tens of thousands of years before European settlement.

The fact that O'Connor died near where their tradition says that the spirits of the departed leave the coast to travel over the sea to the island of the dead, lent credence to this belief.

Perhaps it is true O'Connor was cursed – but not by the Noongar people. For the statue seems symbolic of a culture driven demented by its destructive fever for gold, which fuelled a rush to ransack the natural world.

Leaving one Irishman with many monuments to his name – but his sanity all at sea.

Fairy tales help us live happily ever after

Regular readers of this column might notice my propensity for fairy tales. Growing up, I used to plunder the library for their magic, having devoured to dog-eared death the ones at home. I had no wish to graduate to more grown-up genres.

Indeed, I've been accused of writing fairy tales myself, when it comes to my descriptions of the treatment of animals at human hands. If only the ferocious facts behind the atrocities inflicted on our fellow creatures were make believe!

But those who mock these airy-fairy works of fiction clearly haven't read enough of them. Otherwise, they would know that the last thing they are is a soft soap on reality. The stories collected by the Grimm brothers in the 18th century depicted life as generations of European knew it; capricious and often cruel.

The tales were softened over time, but they never lost their edge. Usually the hero has to face his fears, having strayed off the path into, 'a dark wood', as Dante's *Inferno* puts it, before having any chance of picking up a princess.

'If you want your children to be intelligent, read them fairytales,' Einstein said. 'If you want them to be more intelligent, read them more fairytales.'

For fairytales not only feed the imagination, which Einstein considered more important than knowledge, but are relevant to life.

Who hasn't felt like a Cinderella at times, marginalised and unloved, while the ugly sisters of the world go to the ball?

While anyone who has made their vision a reality, despite a lack of support and doses of derision, can surely identify with Henny Penny.

I have had my own experience of The Elves and the Shoemaker this summer. With my cupboard bare, I stepped out the door one morning to find two plastic bags crammed full of vegetables.

I looked up and down the street, in case a caped crusader might be lurking nearby. Then I considered all possible suspects. Number one was the gardener who had employed two pigs to plough her field; perhaps she was thanking me for saving their bacon? But she was eliminated after I bumped into her.

The mystery deepened when it happened again last week, with yet another bag bursting with goodies swinging from my door knob; a sweet little swede, glossy courgettes, and an abundance of divine smelling apples.

But reader, there is a happy ever after, or a happy ever whodunnit, to this tale of a turnip and other pleasing plants. I discovered that my elf was a gardener. Kind-hearted Karen has been gifting many in town with her surplus bounty.

What a Princess Charming!

Why kindness on this Father's Day shows real class

The shops around this country town are full of everything I might need this Father's Day; from cards to books and wrapping paper. All I'm missing is my Dad.

This third Father's Day since the saddest farewell to my father has got me thinking about my Dad's generosity. It manifested materially, being a great provider – especially in present overload at Christmas.

But his big-heartedness went way beyond family to include friends in need as well as friends not yet met, otherwise known as strangers. Though he was shrewd enough to do his research on charities, to make sure his money made it to those who needed it.

However, his positivity and enthusiasm for giving advice backfired when he tried to become a volunteer with The Samaritans, and they felt that he lacked the essential ability to just listen. This hurt his ego. But he was prepared to give it a battering, attending spiritual retreats run by orange-cloaked monks, where he happily mucked in with the washing up.

The diary he kept during the last decade of his life is a poignant mixture of self-reproaches against his failings, for he was an impatient man with a short fuse, and often resolved to be better. By which he meant more generous. And not just with money, but with his time, and with compassion. Ironically, much of his quest to be kinder stemmed from his upbringing in the sometimes harsh and unsentimental rural Ireland of the 1950s, with its severe mix of sanctimonious piety and merciless poverty.

Aside from his own family's precarious financial situation, he saw people so poor that they went barefoot in winter digging – in vain– for frozen turnips. Its society of hypocrites and gombeen men, snobs and cute hoors toughened him.

Yet it was also where the germ of generosity was born, especially in the form of Brother Ryan and his father's great friend, Stephen Dunne. My father always described the latter as having class. Though he was at pains to clarify that the last thing he meant by this was some elevated social echelon or material benchmark.

Class for my father meant generosity of spirit: a giving nature that nurtures and uplifts others.

You can tell people who possess class by the way the world appears brighter after you meet them. They might point out that it's a lovely day, and mean it, while others are focused on the fact that yesterday was nicer.

Like Mary, who's always brimming with goodwill when she passes on her way to work in a nearby pub.

Or the sparkling-eyed girl who beams a smile at the checkout in the supermarket or when wheeling her baby in a pram. Along with Jack who always waits so his little dog can sniff every corner. And Katherine, regularly knocking on the door of a neighbour on her second bout of breast cancer, offering cakes or bread but always kindness.

As my father used to say if something trivial was bothering him: it doesn't matter a damn.

But giving one sure does.

The June weather risks putting us in deep water

People are lighting stoves this weekend as temperatures continue to drop. The only drenching ahead this summer looks like rain instead of sun.

Flooding is a real threat for those with houses built on land that should have been preserved as flood plains. As June keeps bursting out all over, they're hoping their local rivers don't get any ideas about following suit.

I know the feeling. A few years ago, I left my city-centre pad in the thick of Dublin 8 behind, and now I'm living in a country town in the south-east of Ireland. Our crooked 200-year-old house is called 'River Run'.

But there's nothing sentimental about the name. It's not like one of those 'Cherry Woods' where there's neither sight nor sound of cherries. This place is dead literal.

'River Run' is so seriously nestled on the banks of the River Nore that we have to keep an eye on the water level when it rains, in case we need to order in sandbags.

Rain pricks the river's surface just beyond our window. We're especially vigilant on those days when the path leading past the old castle opposite us is submerged. The row of benches disappears and the ancient orchard behind them becomes a duck pond. No one can venture down the flood plain to walk their dogs.

Alone with river and relentless rain, the castle stares stonily back at us. Ducks stand to attention on the river banks day and night, as if on sentry watch.

Not like the two bachelors who lived here in 1947. They were more interested in what to put on their soda bread than the downpour taking place outside.

In those days, the only fancy Smeg fridge to be had was the back yard. One of the bachelors volunteered to go have a root around in the cupboard.

He opened the door and got more than a pat of butter, as the entire River Nore tried to pour in.

Little has changed since that flood, including the lack of a Smeg. Thankfully, so far we've never had the river gatecrash our afternoon tea.

But when the rain keeps falling, we turn into corny cowboys in an old western, checking the river like we're reading it for sightings of 'injuns'. We know a downpour today means a higher river tomorrow, as water drains off the land.

Then the river bank beyond our yard disappears and the house is surrounded. It feels like you're on a ship when you glance out at the rushing water, as if it's the house and not the river that's hurtling downstream.

My neighbour Noel tells me that older people here say a river going down too fast is a bad sign.

But with any luck we won't repeat the bachelors' experience, and have to change our address to 'A River Runs Through It'.

Past meets present in a barbaric moment

The middle-aged tourists in the bus station queue in Cork caught my eye. The Latin American woman wore a blue raincoat while her African American partner was shrouded in a plastic orange poncho.

Such gear was largely redundant during our sizzling summer. But it was drizzling that afternoon.

The bus wove through streets teeming with people, faces painted red and white for the All-Ireland Hurling Final. It was a red-letter day in the county of the red and white flags.

The tourists also disembarked in Skibbereen. They stood in the deserted street, like two very foreign and forlorn fish out of water as the bus drove away. The man planted a Stetson on his head as he looked around the GAA-induced ghost town.

I wished them a good stay and he told me that they were going on to Baltimore because his name was Jean-Marie Baltimore. He was a retired teacher from the Caribbean island of Guadeloupe. They had come to Ireland as part of their honeymoon just to visit there.

I directed them to a nearby hotel to phone for a taxi. But I spotted them still wandering about in the rain as my friend and I were driving out of town.

'Baltimore!' I called down the main street of Skibbereen to them. 'We'll give you a lift to Baltimore.'

On the way Mr Baltimore told us how he and his bride, Brazilian psychotherapist Bena, had met on the internet six years before. He also spoke about his many offspring scattered across the world.

Did Bena have children? 'Not yet!' Mr Baltimore answered in his deep voice. He patted his substantial stomach. 'Maybe I'm carrying it!'

The car was full of his belly laughter as we careered along empty roads. We reached the outskirts of Baltimore to find a checkpoint in place. The garda told us that we would have to go around Lough Hyne.

So we wound our way through insanely lovely scenery, like something out of a Grimm fairytale, with dripping foliage, ferns, and virgin forest towering above us. At any moment you could expect ogres or trolls to appear.

Mr Baltimore thought we were joking when we told him about the terrible night in 1631, when pirates from the Barbary Coast stole away the inhabitants of Baltimore.

Until we arrived in Baltimore and he saw the castle looking out to sea. Only then did he realise that, after 400 years, he had possibly come home.

They booked into a hotel. We left them waving after us, all smiles, before Mr Baltimore wandered off in his plastic orange poncho to explore his roots.

In the name of fathers both near and on the far shore

Many moons ago, a short story I wrote called *Holy Ghosts* was published in the now defunct *Sunday Tribune's* Hennessy New Irish Writing. A mantra that featured throughout – 'in the name of the father' – was the title of a film by Jim Sheridan a few years later.

They say nothing is wasted. And that life comes full circle. But this Father's Day falls too soon for me to feel happy talking about ghosts. For it is less than a month since my dad passed away.

Regular readers might remember my occasional tales about this man from the backbone of Ireland. One story in particular featured a five pound note that he and his mother lost but then miraculously found on a byroad to Mullingar.

However, it's a piece of fruit and not a fiver that best sums up my father. His habit when he fancied an apple was to first ask if anyone else wanted it. This would go on for some time, as he double and even triple checked. Even after all that, he would only eat half the apple – in case anyone changed their mind.

On that note, he would happily dine on rice and lentils when on retreats. But he relished nothing more than a slab of dead animal on his plate. He would point it out to this 'meat is murder' madam, marvelling 'isn't that fantastic? Would you look at the size of that?'

Maybe he was winding me up, for he was always a joker. Likewise, he would equally terrify and thrill us with supernatural tales from the country. Especially Jack O'Lantern, whose light could lure you ever deeper into the bogs, thinking it belonged to a welcoming host, till you were lost forever.

No doubt such ghost stories thrived in the hell and brimstone atmosphere of 1940s' Catholic Ireland of his childhood. Though my father questioned and ultimately rejected the religion of his birth. Not least for its tradition in those days of reading out contributions at Mass, thus naming and shaming the very poor.

This free-thinking entrepreneur started attending Church of Ireland services, the religion of his best friend. He was also partial to slipping into Quaker meetings, hugely admiring of the lack of pomp and ceremony, and the fact that any member of the congregation could get up to speak if they felt so moved.

He finally committed to the Unitarian Church but also tried to practise Buddhist beliefs, such as loving kindness and compassion. He twice stayed in Plum Village, a community established by the Nobel Peace Prize winning monk Thich Nhat Hanh, who was active in the anti-Vietnam War movement.

Right up to his mid seventies, this man from the Midlands was mixing with monks at retreats in Jampa Ling in Cavan.

Now he has crossed to the far shore. I imagine him there, waving back at me, still smiling.

For a father is no ghost, but ever a guiding light.

Muzzling majority to make money from misery

Whether it's fact or fiction, a good story means you may have your hunches about how things will turn out – but you don't know for sure. That's what keeps you reading.

Life isn't so different. Like the time as a child when I was on a country walk with my family and I was trailing behind. I wandered into a semi-circle of hedges, maybe because I was upset about something.

There I was, crying my little head off, when suddenly I heard a rustling sound. I turned and saw a hare pop its head up out of the hedges, his long ears pointing.

He looked at me, as if to ask: 'What the heck is all the hullabaloo about?'

The sight of that beautiful creature certainly stopped my tears in their tracks.

I have never forgotten the hare that heard me cry. But sadly, I've heard far too many of them crying since then, in footage taken at hare coursing centres around this country – which remains one of only three in the western world that allows this blood sport.

And along with the ongoing loss of habitat, their suffering is set to continue. Until one day, this iconic animal that is the stuff of Irish legend – Oisín promised never to harm a hare – will be silenced forever.

For the blocking of a ban on hare coursing last month (*June 2016*) by not just our Government – but all our major political parties – was a disgrace to democracy.

And it revealed just how powerful are the minority who muzzled any other possible outcome. They wage a war on our wildlife not only in pursuit of a perverse pleasure – but more importantly, because of the profits from the gambling and corporate sponsorship that comes with it.

No wonder the coursing clique kept quiet during the brief furore. Because they knew a ban was never going to happen. And they were right. By imposing the party whip (appropriately enough) our so-called public representatives ensured this blood sport won the day. Maureen O'Sullivan could have performed somersaults, instead of wasting her breath debating the issue to a near empty Dáil. For the die was cast.

Some of the arguments against a ban would have been laughable, if vulnerable hares weren't at stake. Like the gem from the minister who issues the licence to trap, cage and torment these solitary creatures that 'it would drive coursing underground'.

So why ban anything?

Other politicians claimed 'the highest animal welfare standards are in place'.

Really? What about the relentless reports of deaths and injuries?

It's been over 20 years since the last attempt to ban hare coursing was similarly blocked. Since then, Ireland has moved on, to the extent that we now have gay marriage.

Are happy hares just too radical for us?

But the majority in this country who want a ban on this barbaric blood sport don't have to accept this mockery of democracy. If they contacted their TDs, demanding a genuine vote on the issue, I wonder what would happen?

We'd have to wait and see how life turns out.

The highwayman who took the high road

The sun sometimes shines even during showers, these late August evenings – which is when I wander up to a hilly area with beautiful vistas of this country town, to pick blackberries for my breakfast.

The ancient woods there are full of rustling sounds, which mostly turn out to be a bothered blackbird scratching around for sustenance. But it's easy to imagine the days when a traveller would have been terrified in case the trembling leaves suddenly unleashed the infamous figure of James Freney – a highwayman who plied his trade on the roads of Kilkenny, until the end of this month in 1748, when he was given an ultimatum to surrender or else face a charge of high treason, which carried the death sentence.

And while the centuries have rolled on since his robbing, the landscape where he lived has not changed that much. Indeed, Ballyduff House looks almost the same as when its landlord paid for the education of a servant couple's son. No doubt both parents and prospective employer had high hopes for the likeable lad. Though Mr Robbins probably didn't reckon on young Freney following in his footsteps quite so literally, by becoming a Mr Robbins of the rural gentry.

Blame it maybe on Freney's blood, since his ancestors were descended from a noble line with links to the kings of France. A fondness for the good life, without the means to enjoy it, seems to have soldered this gentleman robber.

Locals loved this cad, who was so soft-hearted when it came to looting the ladies that he often returned their jewellery if they grew tearful. While he made sure his victims had enough money to hoof it home after the hijack.

Freney didn't take his thieving too seriously. But it was this cavalier attitude to crime that turned him into an outlaw, after he carelessly let his face be seen when trying to rob a frequent visitor to Ballyduff House. From then on, this robber was on the run.

So it was just as well he hadn't run out of charm, for many folk were willing to shelter him. This allowed Freney to establish a network of helpers, and hence carry on nicking.

Until, that is, the authorities caught up with Freney's fan club and piled on the pressures to reveal his whereabouts via threats of torture and hanging. A reward of £100 was an added incentive. Some say Freney betrayed his bandit of brothers to save his own skin.

The other version has a virtuous Freney trying in vain to save his closest companion, James Bolger, before managing to escape.

Whatever the facts, it seems this highwayman had friends in high places, for Freney kept his freedom. He lay low for a few years, during which time he wrote his autobiography, before reinventing himself as a sort of customs officer at the port in New Ross – where the only hold ups were due to rural rush hours.

And merchants having to stand and deliver their cargo for this former highwayman's approval.

When Sunday is a day of rest and of reckoning

Sunday is the last day of our week, though North America, Canada and Australia view it as the first of the fresh onslaught ahead. That military metaphor being appropriate for those of us who spend life locked in combat with things from careers to childcare, waging a war with work or killing time till we can be with (or away from) our families.

Tough, eh? But as Scarlett O'Hara might say, 'tomorrow is another day'.

That's if it's not gone with the winds of war, specifically World War I in the case of Irishman Frank Gunning, who kept a diary of his week for this time frame just over 100 years ago – after this 21-year-old from Enniskillen, Co Fermanagh, left his job in the banking sector to enlist in the 7th Battalion of the Royal Dublin Fusiliers.

Which is how he ended up in the trenches at Gallipoli on August 12, 1915, where the soil was so sandy it kept falling in. Grateful for the stretcher bearers and courageous Captain Paddy Tobin, who tied a handkerchief around a flesh wound and carried on.

The week that followed included endless treks down the beguilingly named Chocolate Hill in search of water, no matter how filthy, and marching over the shallow graves of fallen comrades.

He got to wash on Tuesday at Shrapnel Gully, his sergeant showing them how to scrape the dirt off their bodies by rubbing them with sand.

But the whistle warning them to keep their heads down blew continuously on August 16. And the great excitement when the mail arrived the next day was as short lived as the lives of over 100 of the soldiers in his battalion, after the surprise attack on August 18. The men catching bombs and flinging them back were soon killed.

As was Paddy Tobin, who led the charge over the ridge brandishing his revolver. 'The second he fired, he fell back, gave one kick, and not another sound. I saw no one return.'

One of the dying that filled the trenches next to Frank that day lay flat on his back, a big slice of his shoulder and neck blown clean off. He kept 'moaning for water, while the sun straight above beat down in a most unmerciful way.' Meanwhile, half the head was blown off a body hanging over a nearby rock, the tunic black with blood.

'You can read of these things,' Frank wrote, 'but there it was straight in front of me. Don't know now how I stood it, it's a wonder I didn't go mad with the awful heat, and everything included. I first felt the dysentery.'

And however your evening might be, Frank spent his in a dug out, looking at the sinking sun and thinking of home, and the heavy losses and pals who were missing, trying not to cry.

Frank was hospitalised the next day. When he was well enough, he was sent back – only to be killed, age 22, on the first day of the Battle of the Somme.

Which was a Saturday; for some the last day of the week before the new week to come.

But that for Frank would neither end, not ever again begin.

We need to keep it country for all rural residents

The fields are full of hay rolls sealed in black plastic that shines incongruously in the sun – for modern farming has come a long way from haystacks and scythes.

And next August (*2017*) could also see hedge-cutting, as Minister Heather Humphreys pushes to extend the existing half-year allowance that conservationists warn will wreak havoc for our wildlife. But feedback from farmers and other rural residents about my recent article addressing this issue makes for interesting reading.

Aside from those comments that dismissed my points as the 'usual enviro lobby crap'. Or assumed I think 'I live here, so you should make the place look nice for me, as I have lost touch with agri realities'.

Maybe it's agri realities that have lost touch with the natural world, given how many disagree that the primary purpose of hedges is 'the security of field boundaries'.

As one farmer put it: 'To have a good farming country, we also need to have a good wildlife country.'

Another complained that 'the Irish countryside is increasingly looking American, with wide-open fields with no hedges. Not good for the environment; not good for wildlife; not good for balance.'

Many farmers care about our fellow creatures.

'I grow a lot of hawthorn around my land and leave them for a few years,' says one. 'They attract our native fauna, from bees, rabbits – even the bats like them in the evening for feeding on flies.'

'The quality of the countryside from a wildlife perspective is nowhere near what it used to be,' another believes. He 'always ran a good few beehives…and it's getting harder the whole time to get spots to put them in, with good forage and yield prospects, between lads cutting ditches very tightly, spraying out all the briars, furze and so on, and rye grass monocultures.'

But it is unfair to put all the blame on modern agricultural practices.

'How many of your neighbours have lawns left uncut?' asked one frustrated farmer. 'How many have whitethorn or blackthorn hedging planted? How many have left clumps of briar to provide food for overwintering animals? How many have daisies in their lawns and let other wildflowers grow and propagate?'

'A lot of people have paved over their front gardens,' another rural resident agrees. 'For myself, I have a nice wild garden and a pond with lots of frogs, as well as a bird feeder that supports families of blackbirds, sparrows and finches.'

Just as well, for our lush landscape is not only critical for tourism – but possibly the future for farming.

'No wonder there have been big declines in so much wildlife,' says another, 'all in the name of producing ever greater volumes of commodity foods that the world doesn't want.'

Especially, as some believe, that farming 'is going to change a lot in the next 20 years in Western Europe; we can't compete cost-wise so a change to high-value, less intensive will happen naturally.'

So best protect wildlife habitats, and not hedge our bets for what lies over the horizon.

Home versus a fearsome fate on foreign shores

My late brother's friend Finbarr talks with yearning about moving home from Western Australia. Who could blame him, especially this early summer, with lush, green pastures full of bovine babies, some no bigger than a dog, grazing alongside their mothers?

But there are also fields of unaccompanied calves, an unnatural and sad sight, although their time as orphans in their homeland is all too brief. For the IFA has reportedly 'worked hard to drive a strong calf export trade' and are pushing 'to develop new markets', such as Turkey, where this month (*May 2017*) more than 3,000 young bulls depart for 'finishing' on local farms.

Which is why this vegetarian finds herself in the surreal position of feeling relief when the slaughter trucks that pass through this country town turn left up the road. That means they are heading to the local abattoir, hopefully for a quick and humane end.

Whereas my heart sinks when trucks go straight towards Waterford, to be shipped to places where animal welfare is an alien concept.

Live exports also leave from Western Australia, where Finbarr says they have moved the ships further from port because the animals are so terrified.

It was the same decades ago. An octogenarian remembers how 'the crafty Freo dockers trained a goat to walk bravely to the top of the gangway – where Nanny/Billy would smartly step aside, while their cousinly ruminants scooted on towards doom. The name given to the decoy beastie? The Judas goat.'

For the betrayal of these gentle bovines is why an emotional debate about live exports has long waged in Western Australia. Like our agricultural minister, politicians there have seen the videos emerging as recently as last month revealing the immense suffering – such as images of animals starving and dehydrated; or cattle hoisted by one hind leg and spun on a chain as a man slashes with a knife at their necks.

So let us remind ourselves of the reality behind live exports: it means shipping live animals to where the only people bearing witness to what happens to them are reputable animal protection groups.

These organisations stress that they are not trying to stop the export of food – but believe it is entirely unnecessary for the animals to be transported while still alive.

'If it was replaced by a trade in meat and carcasses, then the animals would be slaughtered under EU laws designed to protect them from the worst kind of suffering,' says Peter Stevenson of Compassion in World Farming.

This is not some sentimental sideshow. Meat eaters must show mercy and demand limits on the atrocities inflicted on Irish animals by processors and exporters – even if that means killing them with kindness where they were born, rather than abandoning them to a faraway and fearsome fate.

All the evidence about the evils of live exports brings the need for such compassion home.

More than one fly in this summer's soup

There hasn't been much sunshine so far this month, but at least the tepid temperatures means everyone in this country town is enjoying a break from their stove. No need to keep on top of kindling, load up with logs, or to end up fuming when the shops are closed by the time you discover that you're out of firelighters.

So there's humidity, if no heatwave. Which may lie behind the sudden infestation of black flies that yours truly has been floored by over the past weeks.

Forget that joke, where a diner in a restaurant complains about a fly in his soup. Because we're not talking about one fiendish Hans Solo here, but swarms of these irritating insects.

I can't figure out how they're getting in. Living on a river means there is an abundance of bugs just beyond my four walls. But a net over an open window has proven a fairly successful form of pest control – until now.

The beasties are everywhere. Even – quite literally – on television. Even the most thrilling, romantic film is flipped into farce by their inevitable cameo appearance – usually crawling across the hero's nose right at the climax.

Which highlights the fact that one of the worse things about houseflies is how annoying they are. At least most spiders won't bother you for long. Indeed, you can sense the mutual revulsion when they spot you, freezing all eight awful legs before scuttling as far away as possible at the first opportunity.

Flies however are like over-friendly tourists who just won't stop pestering you. They refuse to follow what is surely their own advice and buzz off.

As you soon find out, if you are deluded enough to think they will fly out the door once you kindly hold it open for them.

Instead, like the title of that Clint Eastwood movie, most flies choose to buzz every which way but loose, rather than exiting stage left to life and liberty. And this leaves you standing there like a doorman as an inch-high housefly flagrantly flouts your courtesy.

Instead they choose to repeatedly bash themselves against a window, all accompanied by the less than serene soundtrack of incessant vibration.

Finally worn out, the foolish fly drops dead.

And in so doing, flies remind us of Albert Einstein's definition: that insanity consists of doing the same thing over and over but expecting different results.

Because much as we may hate to acknowledge that we have anything in common with houseflies, don't most of us occasionally persist in battering in vain against an obstacle, growing increasingly frustrated, yet refusing to give in?

Whereas if we calmed down and looked around, we might notice a way out of our worries is right under our nose.

No flies on those who have learnt that lesson.

Up close and personal with a prodigal pigeon

According to quantum physics, there is no such thing as an objective bystander. Which might explain why I'm no longer merely observing the pigeon that I dubbed 'Little Flying Fauntleroy' and have become one of the birdseed Samaritans who feed him.

It was probably inevitable, since I live across the river from where this feathered fugitive waits in hope of getting fed. Sometimes there is no one to oblige and he cuts a forlorn figure, for all his fine feathers.

He often flies to meet me as I'm making my way over, landing on the railings of the bridge and running awkwardly alongside me for a while, before swooping ahead to our rendezvous at the ramp.

I have to say, it's very flattering to be greeted this way; a bit like when strange children or furry creatures take a shine to you – as opposed to trembling or bursting into tears.

It's almost a pay-off for the time it takes to do this good turn. Because providing food is only the first part of doing Fauntleroy a favour. Then you have to become his personal bird bouncer as the plummy pigeon daintily pecks at his *plat du jour*, warding off the crows and rooks that are understandably anxious to snatch some.

I admire their valiant, if futile, efforts. Some of them also give Fauntleroy and his fancy white pantaloons a run for the money in the feathered fashion stakes.

One rather endearing rook sports shaggy black feathers, which make him appear to be wearing a pair of culottes. While Mr Tie-Dyed (as I've nicknamed a batik-styled crow that is also partial to pilfering birdseed from my garden) looks like he's been splashed with bleach.

They may not succeed in stealing seed while this big bird is keeping watch – but they still benefit. For Fauntleroy flies off when he's had his fill, leaving them to feast on his leftovers. That's if the dastardly ducks don't get there first.

These fearless fowls issue some serious quacks when I block their path. Indeed, despite my dire warnings and urgings to scoot, sometimes they just go for it.

And believe me, you haven't seen anything until you've witnessed a duck so determined to dine that it helicopters itself on to the wall before waddling at full speed – beak splayed to suction up as much seed as possible – before a reluctant lift off.

Apparently the fancy fugitive behind all the fuss perches in the back garden of a local in this country town at night. She has dubbed her little lodger 'His Majesty'.

Which should make this pigeon's proper name 'His Majesty, Little Flying Fauntleroy'.

Except that I recently found out that my posh pal was most likely unceremoniously dumped.

This is the fate of fancy pigeons that do not follow orders. Best he doesn't do an ET and try to phone home. For I am told that they would kill this prodigal son.

Making Fauntleroy not so much a rebel as a reject.

Though in the eyes of this up-close onlooker, a very lovely one.

Battle of the buckets for our red-hot sinners

There were more burnt body parts in this country town last week than on the ubiquitous barbecues, as we swapped overcast skies for casting off our clothes. Yes, when a heatwave hits hard, we Paddies respond by hitting back with twice the gusto.

It's no wonder that the summer solstice – which was originally a pagan fire festival – is so popular. We seem to view high temperatures as permission to party.

So maybe that's why we also have a tendency to be hot headed, while a famous case known as The Battle of the Buckets suggests that Catholicism didn't curb our fiery characters.

The incendiary incident happened in the early 1930s, when huge fanfare and parades surrounded the feast of Corpus Christi. Our thoughts in those devout days were not of fun in the sun but rather of pipping neighbouring communities to the post in the Theological Tidy Towns that was the midsummer Corpus Christi procession.

Indeed, a Sacred Heart lamp burned day and night in most homes across Ireland – a constant reminder of the never-ceasing presence of God in our midst.

Not that we let His celestial company get in the way of our less-than-spiritual spats – even when they concerned our attempts to venerate him.

The Battle of the Buckets that erupted in a nearby town – between two feuding groups of females – started because of an unfortunate misunderstanding the day before the Corpus Christi parade. A couple of cheeky bovines being herded through the squeaky-clean streets took a fancy to the ivy wreaths that some hard-working women had proudly made and pinned to their front doors.

Maybe those virtuous viragos were too busy adorning the church altar to notice the cattle chomping away on their delicious displays – for they instead suspected a rival bunch of biddies of being so jealous that they had spitefully mangled their masterpieces.

The fuming females held their fire until the procession and mass were over. Then they confronted their alleged saboteurs when they all gathered to collect water at the Abbey Well.

Dialogue soon came to a (hot) head, resulting in dozens of warring women belting the bejaysus out of each other with their buckets.

A young Philip O'Keeffe, who was picking mushrooms with his pal Sean Holden in an adjoining field, decided to investigate after hearing the loud racket. The two lads scampered home in excitement to alert their parents after witnessing the clashing women.

The battle fizzled out only after the intervention of a nun and a friar, who came running across the meadow, gesticulating frantically to the feisty females to put down their arms.

The pious peacemakers eventually managed to negotiate a ceasefire – but only after confiscating the water-holding weapons.

For we may be a barrel of laughs when the sun is shining – but rain on our parade and we'll make you cry buckets.

Aerial heralds of summer put us in fine feather

You'd need a sense of humour to cope with the weather so far this year. Maybe that's why I thought of the late, great comedian Tommy Cooper when I stepped out into our yard to find the swallows had reappeared. Overnight, apparently. Or as his catchphrase put it: 'Just like that'.

There they were, swooping and gliding to beat the band, as if they'd never left. But these little flying maestros hadn't popped out of Mr Cooper's red fez. They'd actually flown 10,000 km from Africa to soar over this old sod. Swallows earn their wings as members of the jet set.

They put me in flying form too that morning. Because few sights are more uplifting than that of the first swallows. It fills you with optimism, as well as admiration for these fiercely free birds that disdain all feeders. They'll leave the peanuts for the plebs.

Instead, swallows are specialised aerial hunters of tiny invertebrates, catching their prey by keeping their mouths open as they fly through the air. Their long, pointed wings allow them superb manoeuvrability. Flight may be fast and involve a rapid succession of turns and banks when actively chasing fast-moving prey.

Less agile targets are caught with a slower, more leisurely flight that includes circling, and bursts of flapping mixed with gliding.

I'm an 'insectophobe', so their tireless pursuit of creepy crawlies makes swallows my allies. That's a term often associated with war, but maybe that's appropriate. For these intensely independent insect-eaters are fearless.

We live on a river, which is one of their favourite feeding areas, next to their nesting nirvanas of a derelict barn and a bridge. So we're regularly dive-bombed by these gutsy gliders whenever we step too close to one of their high-flying homes.

These winged warriors' snappy appearance matches their midge-munching might. Blue-black upperparts contrast with white underparts, except for a brick-red throat and forecrown. Their long forked tails end in thin streamers, which on the male grow to maximum length during breeding season.

These brave little birds always remind me of kamikaze pilots. Which is fitting. Because not only has the swallow been an influence in the world of aeronautics since antiquity, but two famous Second World War axis fighters took their name from swallows, and remain famous for both their speed and beauty.

While one plane was the Me 262 Schwalbe, the world's first operational transonic jet fighter, the other was called the Kawasaki Ki-61 Hien, an imperial Japanese army fighter.

With such fascinating featherheads around, who cares if 'one swallow does not a summer make'? For their aerial acrobatics can make you smile, even when the sky is grey.

Just like that.

The true location of Moore's last rose of summer

Folk often sit on the bench at the top of this town's main street and watch the world go by. One such regular is Paddy Daly, who is tall and lean like an Irish country Clint Eastwood. Especially as he exudes a peaceable aura of life experience, yet with little evidence of ego or attention seeking.

Which is all the more impressive when you consider that this former gardener for more than 40 years at Mount Juliet (back when it was still a 'Big House' and not a five-star hotel) knows the secret whereabouts of the last rose of summer.

Officially, the blooming inspiration behind Thomas Moore's famous melody is in Dublin's Botanic Gardens, where 'at one time, they had to put a cage around it, as everyone was trying to rob bits of it,' as Paddy says.

This cultivator of the China rose *R. chinensis* 'Old Blush' was raised from a cutting taken from a rose in Jenkinstown House in Co Kilkenny, where Moore often holidayed as a guest of Major George 'Punch' Bryan.

Yet how dried out like the pressed petals of a dead flower does that description sound, after talking to this man who met the last living link to that legendary rose. For the truth is that several offshoots of this fabled flower are scattered about this island.

The last rose of summer even briefly bloomed outside a Kilkenny city pub, until vandalism – not verse – got to it.

Perhaps that was why the guardian of this green-fingered holy grail and great granddaughter of the gardener who tended this bloom that enchanted Moore, entrusted its survival to a kindred spirit.

It seems she contacted Paddy more than a decade ago, when he used to have a gardening show on the radio every Friday. He was talking about roses one night, when this elderly lady rang up and asked him to call into her on his way home.

There, she made Paddy promise not to tell anybody, before giving him several cuttings of the immortalised rose.

'I put them in me pocket,' Paddy recalls.

Five of the cuttings rooted with horticulturist Pat Fitzgerald, who is propagating them.

'You need a certain volume,' Paddy explains. 'It's a slow process.'

Two went to Lissadell House. 'Constance Cassidy wrote me a lovely letter, in her big handwriting, thanking me.'

Another two are in pots in Paddy's garden. Seemingly unaware of the irony of his words, he tells me that the last rose of summer doesn't last long.

However, the flowers keep repeating. 'That's one good thing about them. Some roses have only one bloom.'

It even seems possible that the original last rose of summer could last forever, flowering for all seasons, unnoticed, where that old lady used to live.

'I passed there a few years ago and saw this rose in flower. The people who own that cottage probably don't know they have the last rose of summer in their back garden.' Paddy pauses. 'That's if it hasn't been uprooted, or bulldozed by now.'

Let's hope the current residents like taking time out to relax and smell the roses.

Why this Paddy is getting prickly about the heat

Local hero pigeon Little Flying Fauntleroy's white feathers blended in beautifully with his surroundings during this year's snowy spring. But being camouflaged possibly played a part in the fancy pigeon's downfall after the thaw caused him to let down his guard and fall prey to a female sparrowhawk.

The white-out landscape of a few months ago is strangely similar to this summer's bleached and burnt-out offering – with little urgency to make hay while the sun shines. For fields around this country town are already spun into dried-out fodder.

Several seasons seem stuffed into one, thirsty trees shedding leaves as if it was autumn. While spring was finally in the arid air, with the 'pip-pip' sound of ducklings and birds feeding chicks, it wasn't so much a case of a bat out of hell as those bewildered flying mammals waking to a world as hot as hell.

There were summery delights, such as children crossing the bridge with wet hair and towels around their shoulders after a swim in the river. Market

Street looked positively Mediterranean, the Blackberry Café advertising iced coffee and air-con, while folk ate al fresco.

But despite the macho posturing of die-hards who denied there was anything peculiar about a double whammy drought and heatwave, the honeymoon ended weeks ago.

For May was nice. And June continuing so was a surprise. But then it was July, and the eerily blue skies and scorching temperatures before noon no longer seemed so nice.

Fire brigades tore about as people stopped wondering if the weather would last 'til the weekend. Some confessed that they preferred being indoors with cooling fans to the relentless high temperatures.

'It's not "Irish",' many locals said. 'But it's OK if you're sipping cocktails on holidays,' added a woman in the air-conned sanctuary of a supermarket.

For we associate heat with going abroad for a break, returning home to grumble about our grey skies. But this was home. And working in it was no holiday. Especially as there was no escape.

Just as chilli actually means something hot, life turned upside down. The weather forecast predicted a possibility of rain in the same wincing tones of bearing bad news – but now because they didn't want to get our hopes up. Nobody wanted to admit nostalgia for soft days, drizzle or even downpours.

For instead of our taken-for-granted 40 shades of green, we saw hues of shrivelled straw. Which is no fun for farmers, who are already struggling to cope with too many cattle thanks to the bloated dairy industry.

And that means more poor creatures are likely to be offloaded as live exports to sweltering climates with no animal welfare – especially with claims that meat processors are exploiting the situation by slashing prices further.

Which is why, at the risk of being pigeon-holed as a sun-hating Paddy, when it comes to weather, I'm all burnt out.

Beware of brutal rural Rambos in the night wood

August is upon us – literally – for the weight of the year is now tipping towards darker days. And not just for us, because this month marks the advent of 'autumnal hunting' as fox hunters refer to setting their hounds on vixens and their cubs in preparation for the season ahead.

Though who knows what killed the three cubs that I came across recently, all lying on the side of the road within a mile of each other, distinctive black paws lifeless?

Maybe they were hit by cars, despite their supposed cunning, or were scared out of a field by huge farm machinery, what with combine harvesters currently a common sight. Or perhaps they dashed out in a desperate attempt to escape a gun.

For shooting foxes is considered so unremarkable that a local once told me a story with an aside about a fox straying into a car park and a man responding by taking a shot at him.

The poor fox wasn't the only one who was blown away, for I was shocked by the casual contempt and impulse to annihilate a little animal.

Slapping the tag 'vermin' on these persecuted little predators can make a virtue out of the vilest acts of aggression towards them.

Like lamping – where rural Rambos use off-road vehicles and high-powered lights to locate wild animals at night, before shooting or setting their dogs on them. These brave boys often wear camouflage when in combat with fierce rabbits and foxes. Though sometimes they turn out to be the babes in the wood.

Like a gang recently caught lamping deer. Apparently, they didn't realise that it was cruel to set dogs – especially bred to be big and vicious – on deer – just as they hadn't a clue that it was illegal to lamp a deer in the first place.

Which must explain why they only received suspended sentences for causing unnecessary suffering on a dozen deer.

For lamping is – apparently – not about having a loutish laugh while terrorising defenceless creatures.

We're often told that these armed vigilantes against vermin only tear around rough terrain in their high-powered vehicles in an attempt to help vulnerable ground-resting birds, pheasants and grouse, as well as farm animals, by keeping down fox numbers.

The National Association of Regional Game Councils (NARGC) is campaigning against a proposed ban restricting night-time hunting or shooting that has been recommended by the National Parks and Wildlife Services.

The ban would restrict attacks on wildlife between midnight and 6am from September to March.

Never mind the relentless human encroachment on wildlife habitat. Or intensive farming. Forget the epidemics of feral cats, or of mink escaped from fur farms that wreak havoc on wildlife and farm animals alike.

Just keep pointing the finger at the fox, so we can indulge trigger-happy fingers and allow the hearts of darkness to continue killing under cover of night.

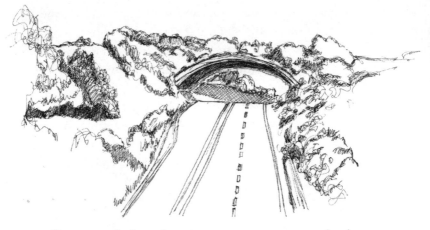

Our whizzing cars are wiping out our wildlife

Rumpelstiltskin, that ferocious curmudgeon of fairytale fame, must be busy spinning this late August, for fields of hay are gleaming like gold. But such fine views are marred by the sight of so much road kill.

It is impossible to drive even a short distance without seeing hedgehogs wiped out at every turn. I saw four pulverised prickly parents on one recent trip, their only crime trying to feed their hoglets and find enough food to stock up for winter hibernation.

Countless other creatures fall victim to the fury of our vehicles. I regularly see runover rabbits, foxes, hares and badgers. While most of us are inured to the sight of dead crows, feathers fluttering forlornly on their lifeless bodies. Even those craftiest of critters fail to deal with cars travelling at over 100kph.

How could they? If you have ever broken down on a motorway, as I did last month, you quickly realise just how dangerous and hostile an environment it is. The breakdown assistance urged me to climb a nearby hill for safety while I waited for help to arrive.

As for those signs that you see on some stretches, warning that deer are about, I often wonder what I would do, when driving at high speed, if one of those Bambis did suddenly jump out. What possible protection does a road sign offer either deer or driver?

Yet it doesn't have to be like this. Luxembourg is the latest country to roll out a series of blue reflectors – the colour of danger for wild animals as it is rarely seen in nature – on their roads, to help reduce collisions between vehicles and wild animals at dusk and at night.

Similar projects in Germany indicate that they reduce night-time accidents involving animals by up to 73%. Germany is not stopping there. Following what has been relatively commonplace in the Netherlands for years, it plans to build more than 100 wildlife bridges over the next decade.

It's largely thanks to a determined campaign by a forester, Gerhard Klesen, who finally convinced authorities that man-made barriers, which restrict animals' natural movement, limit genetic diversity. This in turn leads to an increase in disease, and shortened lifespans.

The 'Green Bridges' are designed to counteract this effect. Cameras set up along them have captured a veritable Noah's Ark of animals making their way across the specially-designed terrain. There are strips of sand just for insects, as well as vegetation providing food and shelter to some of the smaller creatures.

Several animals have set up permanent home on the bridge. Others, such as stags, travel back and forth in search of a mate.

Isn't it time we stopped paying lip service to the slaughter of other species, due to human impingement on their habitat?

Let's be humane, instead of behaving like heartless road hogs.

Wallowing pigs and swollen sows in summer

I often cool down during this late June in a local hotel's pool, where, ironically, I also enjoyed the heart-warming realisation that sibling swine 'Samson' and 'Delilah' are also wallowing these warm days, in their case in mellow mud.

Sadly, the vast majority of pigs in Ireland are denied this instinctive indulgence, instead spending their lives confined in crowded, concrete sheds. Making all the more poignant the reminiscences of Julie Lambert, the erstwhile heartbroken pet lamb lover, about the pleasures enjoyed by pigs on her father's farm just a few decades ago.

'I always remember how they would wallow in mud in the summer and how they would be black from it,' she says. 'They would be in the dunlock, where all the slop went from the cowshed and the water would gather; that was their bath. They loved it because it was so nice and cold.'

But Julie's family paid a pongy price.

'Pigs are supposed to be the cleanest animals on the farm – but the state of them! People would come to our home and ask: "What sort of pigs are those? I've never seen a black pig." But it was just the mud!

'Our neighbours had skinny pigs that would go for you. I don't know what breed we had, but they were always enormous!'

One day, Julie was alone in the barn with a particularly swollen sow.

'She was huge, even bigger than usual, and lying on her own and grunting a lot. She looked like she was struggling.'

Julie was very young and didn't understand. But she soon got the shock of her life – by witnessing the miracle of new life.

'Next thing the sow shot out a bairn really fast – just shot it out! I couldn't believe it!' she remembers.

Julie remembers how 'daddy used to sit up all night with her. He'd stay till the last bairn was born and make sure they'd all get suckled. There'd be smaller ones and he'd try to encourage them.'

They also had to make sure that the sow didn't roll over on them. Nowadays, intensive farming prevents this by using farrowing crates. The sow is confined in one before she is due to give birth and stays there until her piglets are taken away, when they are about a month old. The crate is so narrow that it is difficult for her to stand up or lie down.

'That's terrible!' Julie is appalled. 'Daddy would just keep watch. There would be a fierce squeal if the sow did roll over!'

Maybe it's time we 'squealed' about this controversial practice that typically puts productivity and profit first.

Because it may stop the sow from suffocating her young – but at the cost of crushing that poor creature's spirit.

Summer nights learning to fly the virgin nest

The season is no longer sprightly – despite the juvenile robins, blackbirds, sparrows and crows fluttering around the bird feeds in my backyard. For summer is slowly dying – like the bumblebees that I sometimes find lying flat out on pavements around this country town. They can often be revived by carrying them to the safety and sustenance of nearby flowers.

Though all these birds and bees remind me of the X-rated conversations I used overhear when I travelled by bus to and from 'the Big Smoke'. Two girls sitting behind me on one particularly lustful trip giggled and gossiped the entire way about a certain derelict cottage where they would go to canoodle with their respective Romeos.

However, shacking up in old shacks for shenanigans is nothing new, as an older country boy reminded me recently. Back when country towns boasted not only shops, post offices and Garda stations galore, one soaking wet Sunday saw him cycling to the cinema in the torrential rain.

All because 'a certain wan had given me the eye the previous Sunday night!'

His motive wasn't catching that week's offering of *Calamity Jane* – but rather the casting off of 'the much-jeered stigma of my virginity. It was to be many years before I'd discover that my mates talk was so much bull dust – and we were all in the same boat.'

Given his goal, it's no wonder nerves got the better of this brazen bucko as he approached his destination. So he 'nipped into Molly Bulger's pub, and had a few snifters of Paddy – to which I was also a complete virgin!'

Thus fortified, he and his mot went to the movie, where he 'made a reasonable fist of things by offering her a tuppenny Dinky bar – to which she graciously assented. I was on my way!'

Further progress was made at the interval when an ice cream wafer was purchased from Nosey Kennedy. It was accepted – like the Dinky – with a shy, or coy smile.'

Those were the days when the National Anthem was played at a film's finale, after which they started home.

When they reached a barn – aka the intended boudoir – the virile virgin paused, pretending to adjust his bike chain. Then he asked his date if she would 'perchance dally a while in those romantic environs'.

To which she replied with 'a subtle pressure of the fingers – and I knew a certain Bob was definitely my good new uncle.'

So up into 'the sweet-smelling hay' the courting couple climbed. Where the flirty fellow pondered 'what would Clark Gable do, in these circumstances? Or Gregory Peck?'

Unfortunately 'the dropeens of Paddy were catching up fast!' Next thing he knew, 'daylight was peeping in – and my bird had flown! I was mortified, as she spread the tale about what a loser I was!'

Happily, cupid took pity on this chancer. The learner lovers met up again and 'this time, things went a lot better' – leaving this country Casanova as fully fledged an expert as the birds and bees.

Heartless in our disregard for the homeless

It's summertime, as the Gershwin tune goes, and the living is easy. But while the seasons may soften, the struggles of many do not. So I'm reminded whenever I visit 'the Big Smoke'.

If you go by public transport, you might become aware of these troubled souls long before you reach Dublin and other major Irish cities. Largely because outreach services for homeless people and addicts do not exist in rural areas.

But some things have changed, like the almost homely stereotype of the homeless as bedraggled old men. Gone are the weathered faces of vagrants like Johnny Fortycoats, who were fantastical fixtures of my childhood.

These down-and-outs were often viewed as voluntary outcasts. As such, they still belonged – embodiments of what could happen if that part inside us, that we sometimes sense, is given enough rope to hang us, by stepping too far over the edge.

But these days, when bankers and other big-time players are protected and paid off by imposing penalties on the rest of the community, we start them young on the road to ruin. Reflecting just how far our society itself has wandered into the abyss.

For, only a few decades ago, it would have been inconceivable to passively witness another human being lying destitute on the street. Now, the experience is obscenely commonplace.

As is the spectral sight of the seemingly walking dead, their prematurely aged faces shockingly gaunt, sleeping bags draped like cloaks around skeletal frames. They wander like hungry ghosts from a Tolkien novel among day-trippers and tourists.

Apart from their immense suffering, what is the moral cost of this surreal scenario on so-called functioning citizens, as we learn to become inured and indifferent to their piteous plight? What has happened that we seem oblivious to these broken bundles of humanity at our feet?

It's not that we don't care. But most of us are struggling to make ends meet. Plus we all know about professional beggars and their scams. While the taxes we pay and the public servants we prop up with pensions and power are supposed to look after our most vulnerable.

Like the homeless man I recently encountered in one of our capital's luxurious locations, pushing a shopping trolley piled high with bags of rubbish that constituted his worldly possessions. Perched on top of it all was a little dog who looked grateful to belong to someone who did not.

The man was so stressed out by a recent run-in with a garda that he started talked to me as if we weren't strangers. What worried him most was what would happen to the dog if he were arrested. Would someone mind him? Would he get him back?

Because life can't be easy when man's best friend is, in fact, your only one.

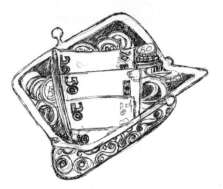

Why miserly people end up paying the price

Australia is currently in the depths of winter, making it a good time for my late brother's friend Finbarr to be visiting the old sod, prompted by a cousin's wedding. He's not only getting a second slice of summer but also saving a fortune on fuel bills.

That's an unlooked for perk in his case. But some tight-fisted folk arrange their lives so they spend as little as possible. Not because they are broke – usually far from it – but motivated by meanness.

For while generous souls would give you the shirt off their back, cheapskates would cram all their clothes in the coffin with them rather than let anyone have them for free.

Many Scrooges only follow the latter part of the 'give and take' equation. They are out for what they can get and exploit less grasping souls. It's nothing to admire, which is why we give credit to a giving person, but no one talks about a taking person.

Misers are especially opportunistic when it comes to social situations. They love funerals – thanks to the free food – but give weddings a wide berth (as they entail a present). You can bet their beloved bottom dollar that any gift will be offloading something they didn't want and no one else would either. But that's another saving in bin bags.

These penny pinchers tend to disappear to the bathroom just as the bill arrives. The fingers of frugal females seem suddenly frozen as they fumble for their purse, so you have paid by the time they prise it open. While mean men opt for the classic scenario of forgetting their wallet.

Far from believing it more blessed to give than receive, they tweak another biblical saying to 'blessed are the mean, for they shall inherit the earth.'

Because it turns out that the line about those with the least giving the most, while those with the most are the meanest, has substance – according to a study of charity in America. It found that the poorest people donate the greatest percentage of their income.

'The rich are way more likely to prioritise self-interests above the interests of other people,' according to Paul Piff, a social psychologist at the University of California, Berkeley. 'They are more likely to exhibit characteristics that we stereotypically associate with, say, a******s.'

However, Piff adds, 'it's not that rich people aren't generous. They're often just isolated. They don't see a lot of poor people in their daily lives.'

This suggests that having all the money in the world can turn your life into a small and paranoid prison, albeit with the most expensive fittings. For you are trapped by distrust and the terror that others – not just strangers but also family and friends – want to steal from you.

Call it karma or the topsy-turvy truth, whereby the opposite is the reality of what ostensibly should be the case. It sounds like the wealthier you are, the more impoverished your life can be.

And that might sound hard to take.

No frills or fluffies – but plenty of spin and suffering

One of my favourite songs is *She Moved Through The Fair.* But while I mooched about the fair near this country town, I spent most of my time admiring the sweet faces of a barn-full of Dexter cows.

Some might say that is typical of a 'fluffy' – a term used to mock supposedly airy-fairy animal lovers like myself. Which is kind of ironic. Because when it comes to live exports, the Department of Agriculture and vested interests remind me of John Lennon's *Imagine,* the way they prefer fantasy to facts.

Many in the industry also stereotype concerned citizens as animal rights fanatics. And while some protestors could possibly be deemed imbalanced, surely the real extremists are those so desperate to push their agenda that they deny the evidence before their eyes, dismissing footage from reputable animal welfare organisations as being staged.

ICSA (*Irish Cattle and Sheep Farmers Association*) president Paddy Kent has even claimed there is 'some sort of vegan plot'.

Yet not just far-out vegans but rural folk fed up with being branded with the same brush are among those watching what is actually happening to thousands of Irish animals at our ports and on foreign shores.

'They think the public are thick and don't know what's going on. But I'm not one of those fluffies who says animals shouldn't be kept, and all that.

I'm pro-farmers. People are entitled to make a living,' says Jim, who grew up on a dairy farm. 'My father was amazing about welfare and I loved being totally involved.'

He may not agree with animal rights, but he is passionate about their welfare.

'Some say "look at all the poor children". And I know that. But someone has to speak up for the animals.'

Which is why he's a loudmouth when it comes to live exports.

'I remember one day I was getting hay for my horses when two trucks pulled up alongside me, turning right for Rosslare. Even at that stage the little calves were bawling their heads off. It was just dreadful. And I said, "I'm going to have to go down to the port and see what's going on".'

What he found was an atmosphere 'like the USSR' which helped him form his own beliefs about live exports.

'There's an awful lot of spin. They're pushing live exports and trying to frill it up. The department keep repeating their mantra about "loaded under supervision" and so on, which appeases people. They think: "Oh, sure, the department has rules and regulations, so of course they're looking after them." But I don't believe they are.'

He has had frustrating experiences whenever he tried to get information.

'I can't tell you the number of people who say "Oh, sure, the calves are really well looked after and get fed and everything." And I say "Really? Why don't you go down to Rosslare and see exactly what's going on and then come back to me?" They keep saying "I imagine this and I imagine that." And I tell them – get some facts. Don't bother imagining.'

And they may say I'm a dreamer!

AUTUMN

Reasons to preserve more than blackcurrant jam

The commuter belt continues to extend its tarmacadam tentacles. But sometimes rural folk themselves don't preserve their way of life. Nearby, a pretty road of cottages bordered by stone walls now faces a sprawling, unfinished housing estate. Further up, they're bulldozing meadows to build a suburbia of supersized houses, complete with automated gates.

'Fair play to him,' one local says, about the farmer who did well selling off the land. But my faith in country people who cherish their heritage was rewarded when I happened upon a farm shop last week.

It was a beautiful afternoon, so I took time off. Deep in the countryside, I spotted the shop sign beside a wooden shed. The door was wide open. There were free-range eggs, beetroot, onions and jars of blackcurrant jam. An old tin full of money acted as a self-service cash register.

I was considering my selection, when a tiny dynamo of dog came bounding up the yard. He stopped at a distance, leaning down on one foreleg and wagging his tail so ferociously that his entire barrel-shaped body shook. Finally he threw his head back and howled.

A man emerged from the house and waved. Then he ambled up the yard, blue eyes crinkled in an easy smile and his skin flushed with good health. Pat Croke has lived around these parts all his life. And it's where he intends to stay.

'I couldn't bear to live in a town,' he said.

The Jack Russell rolled over for pets as Pat told me about the new venture farm shop. It also sells produce from neighbours. So it's a bit of a country co-op.

'That's Glenn,' Pat pointed to a collie loitering down by his house. 'He's probably 16 now.'

Glenn ignored all calls and whistles to join us. But when Pat's son arrived back with another collie, Glenn approached to show me his lovely, greying face. He was nearly at my side, when I unhooked my sunglasses. Immediately, Glenn did an about-turn

'He thought your sunglasses were a camera,' Pat explained. 'Glenn hates having his photo taken.'

I was digesting this when a potato landed at my feet. The younger collie was crouched in position.

'Ah yes,' Pat laughed. 'Alan loves playing potato.'

So I ended up throwing an increasingly saliva-drenched spud, which Alan mostly caught with his mouth. Inevitably, the potato split in two. At which point, it's fair to say that it was a game of two halves.

There was a reminder of 21st-century rural life when Pat used his mobile to check on the cattle. When his son led a mother and her calf into a neighbouring field to join the rest of their herd, I realised that we had talked till the cows came home.

So I wound my way back down the country roads to do the same.

Dishing the dirt on keeping death from the door

It may give you the chance to enjoy living the good life, but moving to the country provides no magic elixir for immortality. Sadly, people get sick and die here, the same as they do in cities.

However, there does seem to be an awful lot of long-lived folk in these parts, with the oldest man in this town aged over 100 – and still living independently.

Most older folk around here are likewise active and outgoing – which no doubt plays a part in their longevity. It certainly isn't always due to following modern health-and-safety standards, as the tale that one local told me about her father and his friend proves. Where, if anything, it seems a case of what doesn't kill you makes you not only stronger, but also live longer.

Her father's friend passed away last year, just a few months shy of reaching his centenary. A bachelor who shared his home with copious cats and dogs, the place was so filthy that this woman's father used to bring his own cup, wrapped in a pile of kitchen paper, for when his less-fussy friend made him a hot whiskey.

The woman always chided her fastidious father for doing so, accusing him of having a brass neck. Maybe so – but surely better a brass neck than a bout of botulism.

After all, the bachelor would eat his sausages straight from the pan, dunking his bread in the lard before it set. Then he left the pan on the stove for the dogs to lick clean.

One evening, the bacteria-loving bachelor was off getting something in another room. The woman's father had just set his glass down next to him at the cosy fireplace – when a cat hopped up and deposited something best reserved for the kitty litter right beside his glass.

Horrified, the woman's father grabbed one of the old *Ireland's Own* magazines that were hanging up around the fireplace.

He whacked the dubious deposit away and sat right back down; as relieved as the ill-mannered moggie clearly was.

Until, that is, the bachelor returned and saw the much-loved magazine on the ground.

He promptly picked it up and slapped down the *Ireland's Own* – covered in the cat's odious own – right beside his friend's glass.

Fortunately, such unsanitary shenanigans didn't affect their bromance, which continued after the bachelor finally had to move into a nursing home, where it emerged that another factor in his longevity may have been due to his never having slept in a bed.

Instead, he had a lifelong habit of curling up in a chair. Probably because he used to be a cattle dealer, who had to be up very early to get the cattle to mart.

So for the last few months of his life, the nursing home staff let the bachelor continue to kip on a cushioned bench.

It seems there is no sleeping on the job when it comes to enjoying a long life.

It's time for foxhunters to get off their high horses

As 'Lay of the Land', I'm a dish served up on a platter of print in the *Sunday Independent* every week. Unfortunately, some diners have developed moral indigestion, with the Hunting Association of Ireland (HAI) suggesting that my 'rural' column falls foul of the Trade Descriptions Act.

This criticism was made following a piece I wrote about 'cubbing', as foxhunters refer to their 'sport' of setting packs of hounds on fox cubs.

Well, pardon me, but this isn't something you're likely to see on any city high street.

The situation I outlined is accurate.

Maybe the HAI, being the national body that coordinates and promotes hunting with hounds, just doesn't like me saying things the way they are.

Allow me the same liberty to measure their 'sport' against the Trade Descriptions Act. For most people, sport is generally a contest between a willing set of players, who compete on a level playing field.

How does that match up to people on horseback and foot, armed with whips and packs of hound, blocking up an unwilling opponent's escape outlets in advance? Or trapping hares and forcing them to endure trauma and potentially fatal injuries from being chased by huge dogs?

However, foxhunting does introduce a novel phenomenon to the athletic world.

Move over 'bad loser' and say hello to 'rotten winner'. What other 'sport' defines victory by ripping its opponent to shreds?

As for privilege, I wield no greater weapon than an ageing laptop.

What about the foxhunter's privileged position on his high horse, or armed with guns?

The HAI believes blood 'sports' are justified because they're a tradition 'that goes back through history for centuries.'

So what? So did witch hunts and slavery.

You know what else is a tradition? Standing up for the underdog.

This is especially relevant, now that animals have been recognised by EU law as 'sentient beings' that can suffer and feel pain.

Hunters may 'live for their weekend hunting.' But should that give them the right to allow suffering animals to die for it?

All my columns are not about animals. But strangely, the HAI doesn't seem to find these other pieces noteworthy.

Here's the deal. I'll write about the proliferation of ragwort, as the HAI helpfully suggest, if they stop giving me reasons to focus on animal cruelty.

Fortunately, like the HAI, I can speak up for myself. It's a privilege we share.

The tragedy is that other creatures on this island cannot.

Equine apples of our eye are cruelly harvested

Branches are heavy with apples, those of the red variety reminding me of an ad for a well-known cider. Joe, who lives up a hill overlooking this country town, welcomed me to the windfalls from his 100-year-old tree. I've been feeding them to horses in a nearby field as a much appreciated treat at sunset.

I wish I could feed even one autumnal apple to those horses that are no longer here to enjoy that most lovely time of evening. My encounters with them were brief but brutal, thanks to the red trucks that all too regularly passed through town during this glorious summer.

I thought at first that they contained battery hens. But then one stifling hot Sunday in July, the sun blasting down while birdsong filled the air, I noticed one waiting at the corner ahead of me.

Though some distance away, I could hear the stamping noise of hooves coming from inside. Then the truck turned out on to the road. As it passed, I looked between the slats at its cargo of live horses.

There were quite a few of them crowded in that slaughter truck on that baking hot afternoon. I don't know if they were secured against the twists and bumps of their journey. Maybe it didn't matter if they were injured because of where they were going.

The sun shone from a cloudless blue sky as the truck disappeared down the road, taking with it those nervous-by-nature animals and their sounds of distress.

But I remembered them later that same day, when a luxurious equine coach passed me on its way out of town. Most likely it was heading to the nearby race track.

And it was a coach; you couldn't by any stretch of the imagination call it a truck. It was the sort of bus you could envisage people travelling on. It had a set of open windows all along its length, which was painted a dreamy cream. Clearly the horses within were valued.

The contrast between those two vehicles made me realise that we don't really love horses in this country, despite our protests to the contrary. We only love them as long as we're getting something from them, whether financial or through status or some other form of profit. When that stops, we dump them. From favourite filly and 'my little pony', to a binned and blackened beauty.

That luxury equine coach is the image Ireland likes to project of itself. Not so much a whitewash as a lick of cream-coloured paint. But scratch the surface and you'll find a dirty blood-red reality underneath. And a nation of hypocrites when it comes to its handling of has-been horses.

Because for them, apples truly are the forbidden fruit.

Stolen pleasures are sweetest for princess pirates

This autumnal weather is often wild and windy, with the river beyond my backyard not so much running as racing along. But it was dead calm under a cobalt blue sky when some city friends came calling recently.

They brought two little girls with them, aged five and seven, who daintily nibbled their way through the afternoon tea I laid on.

Later, we took turns kayaking down the river. But the highlight of that delightful day was watching those petite princesses react to the rumour that pirates sometimes land on the sandy end of the riverbank, leaving behind titbits of their stolen treasure.

Because before you could say 'nice dress!' or 'I prefer ankle socks with lacy trims', those little ladies had turned into the savviest pair of ransacking smugglers I'm ever likely to meet, ruthlessly scouring the stones on that sandy beach for said goodies.

First one found sovereign coins, then the other priceless jewels. 'Can I keep this?' was the big question. With the answer an affirming 'arr!', you couldn't drag the determined darlings away from dredging for more delectable debris. Only when satisfied with their caches did they deign to accompany the adults home.

For the rumour was based on reality, with pirates operating in the busy sea-lanes off the south coast of Ireland during the 16th, 17th and 18th centuries. They were attracted by the huge growth in trade between Tudor England, Ireland, the Indies, and the Americas.

The Saltee Islands dominated the sea approaches of the richly laden merchant vessels, making them ideal bases to go plundering. Pirates used the island caves as storehouses for their ill-gotten gains. They included the 'Biscayners' – Frenchmen from the Bay of Biscay – and 'Dunkirkers' from North France.

The most notorious of these privateers was Alexander Vailes. The state papers of that time record how this ballsy buccaneer once boarded a French ship opposite the heavily armed Duncannon Fort, Co Wexford, and pillaged '46 tonnes of wynes which was presently brought by said pyrates to Waterford and there sold to the inhabitants thereof, and other places thereabouts'.

It seems the coastal inhabitants were no puritans either, with many of them not only admiring Vaile's audacity but actively aiding him. The freebooters also did a considerable illegal trade with the local gentry, who were in turn accused of harbouring 'pyrates and of receiving part of the goods robbed by them and stowlen'.

The authorities were convinced, in fact, that many of the cellars of castles in Wexford were stocked with brandy and wine supplied by pirates from the Saltee Islands. Suspected gentry were required to take out bonds to the effect that they would not 'aide, relieve or maintain any such pyrates or in any way intermeddle with them'.

The same might be needed for any future visits to this riverbank of sweet little swashbucklers with a taste for hidden treasure.

The American dream of Frank De Martini

Third-level students from this country town are well ensconced back on college campuses. Many spend the summer in America, courtesy of the J-1 Visa, which has long been a legendary rite of passage.

Maybe that's why I'm thinking of my old pal, Dermot, this eve of the 16th anniversary of the terrorist attacks. He, too, took the J-1 path to the 'Big Apple', back in the day, where he worked on building sites for a Frank De Martini.

That magical name stayed with me till it rang a bell, many years later, when I was watching a documentary on the Twin Towers. But back in those relatively innocent days, Frank De Martini was the dream boss that Dermot met by chance, after an Irish girl working in an employment agency gave him a tip for a job as a carpenter's helper.

'The place was a mess, so I cleaned it up. Frank came in and exclaimed: "God almighty! This is exactly what I want! I mean, I can't think unless a place is exactly like this!" I'm the same so we hit it off immediately,' says Dermot.

Frank 'was so enthusiastic about life. He lived the American dream'.

He was also 'totally fair and a team player who protected his employees. One guy was a photographer, though carpentry was his day job. But he was absolutely useless; another boss would have fired him immediately. But Frank wasn't the vicious type. He had a caring side'.

He also had a brilliant sense of humour, regaling Dermot with stories about his Italian grandmother, who was always going on about how great Italy was, and how America had no class. Till Frank finally went there on holiday, 'and God almighty, Dermot! They had three ducks going up the sitting room wall! So tacky'.

Dermot didn't hear from Frank after that summer, till one night three years later, when the phone rang in his mother's house. 'A friend, Dave O'Sullivan, used to be great at taking off Frank's unbelievable accent. So when this voice came down the line, I was like: "Ah, would you stop, Dave — though that's a great imitation." And Frank kept saying: "No, this is me! How are you doing? When are you coming back over?"'

The zip codes had changed by the time Dermot did and he couldn't get through on Frank's number. The next time he heard his voice was when I played him a YouTube video down the phone of the World Trade Centre's construction manager, discussing the 1993 bombing.

'That's his voice,' Dermot said softly. 'That's Frank.'

Eight years later, on September 11, 2001, Frank De Martini was having coffee with his wife on the 88th floor of the North Tower when the first jet-liner hit. He immediately helped evacuate his floor, before accompanying his wife down 88 flights of stairs.

Then he and a co-worker, Pablo Ortiz, went back into the tower. They were in the 78th floor sky lobby when Frank's last words were recorded: 'Express elevators are going to collapse.'

Frank never made it out and his remains have never been found.

He and Ortiz rescued over 70 people that day.

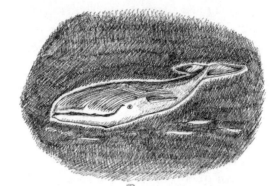

Brutal encounters with ocean's gentle giants

Summer is truly over, for the fish in this country town's river are no longer jumping. Maybe that's why I keep thinking about my trip to West Cork, where I encountered minke whales and dolpins with their calves.

I'm considering a return trip next month, when humpback whales are due to visit. Though nothing can be taken for granted; whales are protected under international law, yet countries like Japan, Norway and Denmark exploit loopholes to continue hunting them to near extinction.

So it's no surprise that my brief encounter contrasts vastly with the brutal one that lit a fire beneath Captain Paul Watson of Sea Shepherd. This marine conservation organization, which advocates 'aggressive non-violence', has a growing number of Irish supporters.

It happened back in the 1970s, when Watson was still with Greenpeace. They detected a Soviet whaling fleet about 60 miles off the coast of California and decided to put their little boat between the 150-foot Soviet harpoon vessel and the eight sperm whales that were fleeing for their lives. Every time the harpoon vessel tried to get a shot, Watson's boat blocked them.

Finally the captain smiled at Watson and drew a finger across his throat. Moments later, there was an incredible explosion as a harpoon flew over their heads and struck one of the whales. She screamed and rolled over in a fountain of blood.

Immediately, the largest whale in the pod threw himself at the harpooner. But they were waiting for him and fired an unattached harpoon at point-blank range. The whale fell back on the water and was rolling in agony when Watson caught his eye.

Suddenly the whale dived, a trail of bloody bubbles hurtling towards them.

'His next move meant he would fall and crush us,' Watson recalls. 'That whale had the power to kill us right there and I could see that the whale understood what we were trying to do. Instead of coming forward, he fell back. I saw his eye slip beneath the surface and he died.'

The encounter changed Watson. 'What I saw in his eye was pity for us, that we could take life so ruthlessly and mercilessly. The Russians were killing these whales and using them for a high-heat resistant lubricating oil. One of the things they were making with it was intercontinental ballistic missiles. So here we are destroying intelligent, magnificent creatures for the purpose of making a weapon meant for the mass extermination of human beings. That's when it occurred to me that we humans are insane.'

Watson feels 'personally indebted to that whale. It's one of the reasons I've dedicated my life to protecting them.'

But the battle between right and malignant might goes on. So don't put off any whale-watching plans.

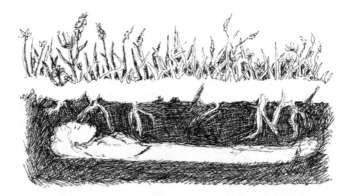

A ghostly tale of the lonely lights of Cloyninnie

The shops in this country town are stuffed to the gills with ghoulish goods this Halloween. But some ghost stories are not so much spooky as supernaturally sad.

Such is the case with this piece of local folklore that was foreshadowed when a neighbor mentioned it, following a tragic local drowning, with an elderly local later filling me in on the details.

It concerns a beautiful young girl called Jenny Butterfield, whose earthly remains from over a century ago lie beneath one of the ancient 'trees of Cloyninnie.'

Jenny was an only child whose mother had died giving birth to her. Despite this, she led a happy life, at one with the flowers and small animals of her home and the surrounding fields. Until the stereotypical evil stepmother entered her life, turning it into one of brutal mistreatment.

According to legend — a local, Kate, who was 80 years old back then, having been born in Famine times — recalled how the stepmother's final explosion of rage erupted when she returned home early one day and found

Jenny dancing around her room instead of drudging downstairs as ordered. A thrashing of savage intensity ensued.

That night, Jenny climbed out of her bedroom window and disappeared. Searches were mounted, Jenny's father walked the country, half-mad with grief. But it was all in vain.

Until a girl skating on an ice-covered pond that Christmas Day started screaming: 'Jenny Butterfield! I saw Jenny Butterfield looking up at me!'

Sure enough, the ice was smashed and Jenny's perfectly preserved body was lifted out. 'She looked as if she was in a peaceful sleep,' said old Kate, who was at the pond that day.

Those were ignorant times, for though there was no evidence that Jenny had taken her life, the parish priest denied her a plot in consecrated ground.

But the farmer who owned the land where Jenny had collected flowers, blackberries and mushrooms agreed immediately to her grief-stricken father's plea that Jenny be buried in that wild and beautiful place. And there on the sunny side of Cloyninnie the little girl was laid to rest.

But sometimes late on summer nights, or during the cold frosts and fogs of winter, the elderly local remembers sitting at an upstairs window with his sister and seeing 'strange lights playing and shimmering around the pond where Jenny had drowned — like little glowworms or fireflies. Then the glims used to all gather and melt into a light about the size of a football. This strange apparition would drift away over the stooks of corn and the tram-cocks of sweet-smelling hay, towards the little grave under the chestnut tree.'

Many locals testified to seeing these phenomena, which became known as 'the lights of Cloyninnie'. But nobody was ever afraid of them — 'because we knew it was only little Jenny's soul, going back to that almost forgotten grave under the kind, sheltering trees in Cloyninnie'.

Telling tales on the country town snitch

People often joke about the village idiot. And certainly there are gombeens galore in all communities. Though to paraphrase Swift's observation on satire, we are likely to discover them everywhere expect in the mirror.

However, dangerous eejits are more prevalent, but no laughing matter. For every country town has its resident snitch.

These modern day followers of 'the valley of the squinting windows' must yearn for the era when religious orders ran this country and ratting was rife. Prattling to the parish priest about which neighbour was enjoying extramarital nookie or had a bun in the oven out of wedlock was a popular pastime for these self-appointed paragons of propriety.

Snitching was still being encouraged as standard practice when I was in national school – with the 'good' girl put in charge of supervising the rest of the class when the teacher left the room. She would happily tell on those of us who misbehaved, smiling piously as we were punished.

That was when children were supposed to be seen and not heard – a practice that today's squealers have adopted to become equally subtle. For these sanctimonious stalkers of their fellow citizens have tailored their technique to the changing times, being champions of the confidential phone line and treacherous tip-off.

Perhaps our history has made us hostile towards those who involved the authorities.

But snitching is a world away from whistleblowing. As the shameful saga of Sergeant Maurice McCabe shows, it takes courage and character to expose corruption. The dire consequences for those who do will hardly encourage others to speak up.

As it is, we often tell ourselves that tolerance stops us reporting abuse of people and animals. When what we call being 'cool' is in fact cowardice, for we fear disapproval and our popularity plummeting so we become pariahs.

Whereas grassing on others doesn't take guts, for those who do so are usually advocates of anonymity. A snitch is the two-face fellow who admires your new shed the same day he phones the council to inquire about its planning permission.

Sometimes they fit the stereotype of retired busybodies with too much time on their holier than thou hands to mind everyone else's business.

Bolstered by a convenient belief that they are doing their civic duty and armed with an aggressive attitude of self-righteousness, they patrol their community, on the lookout for those who aren't strictly keeping to the letter of the law, instead of its spirit. They seek out the pettiest of misdeeds.

Perhaps the spirit of Christmas might encourage these goody two shoes to acknowledge that spite often spurs them on. Before pondering that proverb about people who live in glasshouses.

Because if someone throws stones that smash their windows, will witnesses care enough to tell?

Cemetery Sundays soothe those left behind

A single horse chestnut lying on the ground reminded me of a truism: no matter how strong the sun still shines, this season, like all good things, must come to an end.

Tragically, so too must good people. But remembering them does not, as I was reminded on the first evening of this month.

Hundreds of people streamed uphill, past cars lining every inch of the road. Two older ladies told me they were on their way to a Cemetery Mass.

It happens every year, Billy Davis confirmed when I found him at the cemetery side entrance. As usual, this wiry teetotaller was tanned and smiling, dipping in and out of his local all day for cups of tea between jobs. Here he was again, helping out with the cemetery upkeep collection.

Though it was probably one of Billy's easier gigs, for there was no need for him to say a word. The procession made straight for the plastic bucket, dropping notes in before they climbed over the steps.

Billy asked if Cemetery Masses happen in Dublin. I had never heard of them before. But I discovered afterwards that they take place all over Ireland, often on the first Friday of August.

It hadn't been on the radar of some locals either, not until life gave them reason to take note.

Like Ben Hennessey, who runs a B&B in a gorgeous old tower on Main Street. His beloved wife, Tess, passed away earlier this year. Impeccably turned out, as always, Ben was accompanied to his first Cemetery Mass by his only son, Michael.

Everyone was there, young and old, toddlers to teenagers. There were people with walking sticks and some carrying portable chairs. Many cradled homemade bouquets or pot plants in their arms.

A red-haired boy, still wearing his hurling outfit, hopped out of a passing car. He hurried towards the cemetery, spiky shoes tick-tacking on the pavement, helmet under one arm and hurley in the other.

A young woman followed, one of her daughters clutching a stone with 'Dad' painted on it.

I asked Billy if he had family in there. Oh yes, he answered; his father and brother, cousins.

'And my daughter,' he added, in a quieter voice.

There was no fanfare. No cameras. Just a thousand or more people crowded into a small country cemetery to remember their dearly departed. And to express faith and hope that they rest in His peace.

Mass started at eight, the priest's words pouring out over the congregation: 'Christ have mercy.'

'Bring light to those in darkness,' he intoned. 'Let us pray.'

I left as dusk fell, knowing another day would dawn. For life, like love, goes on.

I'm falling for the ample charms of autumn

It's funny how officially we all love summer, what with its obvious upsides of sunshine and long days. Yet it's almost as if we feel obliged to do so because to feel otherwise would seem somehow odd or even ungrateful.

But while we complain about the cold and rain, scratch the surface of many Paddies — though preferably not after a roasting during that sweltering season — and they will admit, albeit in guilty tones, that actually they prefer autumn.

Why wouldn't they? It's not just our pale skin but also our disposition that means we have a low tolerance for humidity and high temperatures.

Plus our autumn weather is often mild and even warm, even when wet or windy. There are also blue skies and bright sunshine, though without the hassle of intense heat.

And while flowers are fabulous, surely they are no more spectacular than the flaming shades of red, copper and gold as the leaves turn. Speaking of which, what can match the satisfying sensation of crushing a dried out leaf underfoot?

Americans refer to autumn as 'the fall', appropriately enough, as driving down any tree-lined country road reminds you. Leaves flutter surreally to the ground in the barest breeze, making you feel as if you're passing through a beautiful dream.

Which maybe isn't so far off the mark, given that so many religions and spiritual beliefs claim that is all this life is.

Contemplating such cosmic questions and meditating on the meaning of it all — arguably not only a good use of our limited time on Earth but possibly the point of it — is also something that autumn encourages, as the days drawing in likewise draw us towards the stove.

I've started lighting mine, but not till late, because I'm out and about until dusk most days. For I've become more than a little obsessed with blackberries — so much so that I'm unable to go for a country walk without scanning the hedgerows for easy pickings. I whip out the lunch box that I've taken to carrying at all times if I spot any.

Autumnal foraging is a great way to take your mind off mundane matters. It's easy to be in the moment when you're trying to avoid thorns — or failing to do so and paying the prickly price.

Focusing on finding the best berries while birds are twittering all around you also makes the time pass, so you get your fill of fresh air.

Foraged fruit is tastier and more nutritious than the stuff selling for a small fortune in the shops.

But even nature knows that there's no such thing as a free lunch, for my hands are covered in nettle stings and cuts, while my coat has taken a thrashing from getting caught in brambles as I struggle to secure that juicy berry just beyond my reach.

I also have to run the gauntlet of creepy crawlies, midges and dying wasps to get the goodies.

But just as sunburn goes with summer, apparently there's no pleasure without pain. And I'll take autumn any day — thorns and all.

Keeping it kind and keeping it country, too

Visiting Dublin only confirms my decision to move to the country — and not just because it means I'm close to nature. For life here is on a more human scale.

It's the same for my old school friend, Susan, who I met up with recently. She commutes for over an hour to her work in the Mater Hospital. Susan had always loved animals and she told me that she had indeed started training as a veterinarian nurse.

'But I only lasted one day,' she admitted.

First, there was a visit to the slaughterhouse. Followed by a man with a greyhound that wasn't fast enough for racing, so he wanted him put down. Next came a woman with nine mewing kittens.

Susan is still haunted by the sickening lessening in sound as she made her way through that cardboard box, snuffing out nine little souls who got less than 48 hours of life, let alone the proverbial nine. The next morning, Susan switched to human nursing.

That pathetic back story to Susan's change of career also explains why country life can be a double-edged sword if you believe, as I do, that all sentient beings — both humans and non-humans — share a basic right not to be treated as the property of others. Which makes me a modern-day abolitionist, a word that is appropriately related to the social movement that ended human slavery.

For our assumption of superiority over other sentient beings — which basically means any creature who can feel pain or pleasure — that justifies our exploitation of animals, is painfully obvious outside the ironically cloistered environs of cities.

Fields of increasingly adolescent-looking cows regularly disappear to be replaced by more of the same in the intensive system that constitutes modern farming.

While heavily pregnant bovines seem to be forever trudging across the walkway above one particular stretch of motorway I pass.

In many ways, they endure more suffering than other livestock, being perpetually impregnated till they are prematurely worn out. All so that we can continue the dubious distinction of being the only species on this earth that drinks the milk intended for the young of another species.

Above all is the relentless rattling of slaughter trucks along the street, leaving behind the benign, sad smell of cows and sheep. And, of course, discarded horses. All while SUVs with trailers attached and horse carriers head for the nearby racetrack or a day's hunting.

Meanwhile, the abattoir in town corrals animals to their doom as people walk by, either oblivious or else thinking that this is the proper order of things.

Making it all the more ridiculous to me that the 'Repeal the Eighth' campaign rages on, with some locals proclaiming themselves 'pro-life' and others 'pro-choice' — even as they deny other sentient beings the basic privilege of either.

But the steadily increasing numbers of both city and country folk who share my perception adds a heartening new meaning to life on a human scale.

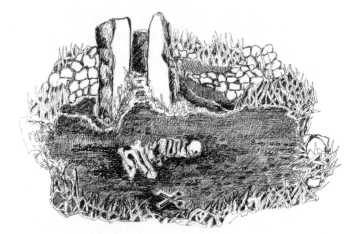

Dark designs as once tailored by Knight De Frayne

Many fields beyond this country town are advertised as sites for sale, even though there is no shortage of derelict buildings lying empty. It isn't just the expense and hassle that means most are destined to become ruins — for rural buyers often want to build a brand new slate.

Unlike the country town cottage heaving with history that I call home. Far from being put off by the countless people who were born and died here, I love the thought of all the previous occupants that have passed through its doors.

Or occupied its windows, as was the case with the resident tailor who used to sit cross-legged in the one that faces the street.

He was lucky to have a space tailor-made for sewing, for many craftsmen in former times had to trudge from one farmhouse to the next in the hope of buttonholing their bread and butter. This left them vulnerable to ambush and attack by highwaymen like James Freney.

Which is exactly what happened a terrified tailor one dark night.

As was the way of highwaymen, Freney plundered the tailor's pockets, but his pleasure at finding his purse soon turned to confusion when he then came across a needle and thread. Realising the man's profession, Freney returned his few coins and bade him a good night.

This was because Freney famously prided himself on being a principled sort of pilferer, only stealing from those with pots of loot. But perhaps he was also tender towards tailors because of the demonic actions towards another doomed dressmaker by his distant relative — the infamous Knight De Frayne.

De Frayne not only abused his tenants but also those who had the misfortune to cross his path. This included a poor tailor by the name of Plunkett, who was employed by the fiend. De Frayne inevitably found fault with the tailor's work. But rather than simply telling him off, De Frayne buried him alive.

Legend has it that while this gruesome act was being carried out, a supernatural voice was heard to exclaim: 'guilfer, guilfer, guilfer.' That is: 'you shall pay for it.'

When the obnoxious knight demanded to know whom he meant, the voice answered: 'Not you, but your seventh generation.'

Emboldened, De Frayne scoffed: 'If it is to go so far, the devil may care!'

The psychopathic De Frayne had a point, for the decline of the De Frayne dynasty only occurred long after his death.

While the spot where the atrocity took place became known as Plunkett's Glen and was shunned by all.

Its fate was sealed after the farmer who owned the field ordered labourers to remove the cairn there. They fled in terror after discovering the tailor's bones buried underneath, along with his trademark pair of scissors.

So don't be deterred if you're considering making a silk purse out of a pig's ear. Old ruins may come with a history of happiness and merriment, along with the crumbling walls.

While the freshest of fields can have a deep dark secret.

Shameful secret of dirty laundry and difficult girls

Leaves are falling, though not for the first time this year; parched plants shedded profusely during the long, dry summer. Maybe it's why it seems ages since Pope Francis's visit in August.

Or maybe it's the change of seasons which is bringing to mind the Papal visit, and stirring memories of how the Pope asked forgiveness, particularly for the abuse suffered by vulnerable Irish women at the hands of the church and State.

For how lightly the latter has got off for its part in our shameful past; as if politicians and other prominent citizens didn't give religious orders carte blanche to persecute the poor for their benefit.

Maybe it's the seasonal change in the sky, the darkness drawing in earlier and earlier, which is bringing into view unwelcome shadows of our darker times.

Because you didn't need to be an unmarried mother to be locked up in the laundry that was run by nuns in this and other country towns. Girls 'from families that had no money would end up there', remembers a local. 'Girls too young to be pregnant; they were just difficult.'

He recalls how every Sunday 'they'd be walked down Station Road, a nun in the front and a nun at the back, all dressed in the same uniform. Can't look left or right; keep your eyes straight ahead. If they saw a man or boy, they'd be in trouble when they got back.'

That was their so-called day of rest. For the other six, society's fat cats had found a profitable solution for these unruly offspring of the poor.

'They'd be cleaning sheets, often from wealthy farmers who wouldn't have changed them for weeks, so there'd be a lot of work. They'd use the mangle and be hanging them all up, sheets and pillowcases, and there'd be other girls ironing and pressing them.'

Among them was his cousin's daughter. 'She was from a huge family and the mother couldn't care for them properly. That daughter was a problem child. So a court put her into the laundry.'

Maybe those high spirits saved her life. Because 'whatever treatment she was getting, she ran away, and where did she run but to my mother? She went upstairs and wouldn't come out'.

'I remember my mother in the room with her arm around this girl. The gardaí came, and someone from the laundry, but my parents wouldn't bring her down.'

The girl fled to England and 'did very well. But she died young, in her 50s.'

Yet that was decades longer than some of the girls who spent their childhoods scrubbing dirty sheets.

'People did die in the laundry. They were buried outside the ditch, in the shankyard. You can see the back of the laundry when the leaves are gone from the trees.'

But even when trees were in bloom, everyone knew it was there. The shedding leaves makes it impossible to ignore. And that, far from being difficult, the daughters of the deprived were all too easy to exploit.

Forcing them to forfeit their family, freedom and often a future in service to — literally — the filthy rich.

Hounded from home to a brave new world

Autumn is beautiful in the country, even during this season's sporadic downpours. For dripping trees sound evocative in the stillness of the landscape, especially in some scenic spots that seem to have barely changed over the centuries.

Like the little townland of Kilcross, where a poor Protestant girl called Jane was one of 18 children born in 1911 to a 'useless farmer'. She had never been further than this town, until the day she travelled the seven odd miles to its railway station.

'We only had a donkey and cart,' Jane remembered, in a recording made by her son-in-law, Roger Buisson, in September 1999, when she was 88.

'I think my sister, Harriet, might have come with us; she was 11. Billy says he came too. My mother drove us there.'

Though what really drove this aunt of a local was religious persecution. As was clear when the interviewer asked about the decision that was made for her to leave Ireland.

'I think the decision was actually made for us by the IRA and the Sinn Feinians,' she replied, without rancour. 'Because it was a very bad time, in 1921, after the uprising. There was civil war in Ireland.'

Jane was about 10 years old and staying in the head gardener's quarters in Flood Hall, one of the many Big Houses that would be destroyed by the war. She went to school from here and helped look after the gardener's wife, who was sick with cancer. Jane's sister was engaged to their son, Bill Graham, who was 'very outspoken. He wasn't a Sinn Feinian; he belonged more to the other side, the English, maybe'.

Which is how Jane ended up sitting on a board on the back of a donkey-drawn cart.

'One of the groups from either the Sinn Feinians or the IRA — I don't know which, I think they were mingled up in the end — they came and took Bill out of the house while I was there. They gave him a bashing and then threw him out the front gate, down the steps onto the grass. I was grabbing at their coat tails and yelling at them: "Don't hurt him! Don't hurt him!" But he was told to get out of Ireland'.

Jane's sister went first. To England, where she got work as a cook in Kent, before finding work for both her fiancé and one of her brothers.

Then it was Jane's turn 'because there was nothing in Ireland for me. They got me a job, would you believe? I was all of 14 – 14 and three months, I think. They got me a job in a house in Putney, to put in my six months there'.

For England was the first step to a new life in Australia. In those days, you had to stay there for six months before migrating.

So Jane went home to Kilcross, 'til another of her siblings, Annie, could come back from her job in England to collect her.

'Because I wouldn't have known where to go. First time I'd been on a train. First time I'd been anywhere out of Thomastown'.

Then Jane said goodbye to her mother. She would never see her again. Nor see another autumn in her homeland, until her life had likewise entered that softly-lit season.

Let's commit to a long-term retail romance

'Something old, something new, something borrowed, something blue,' goes the saying. Certainly, you always know when it's going to rain confetti around this country town, instead of the usual cats and dogs. Notices secured to telegraph poles provide the name of the love-birds about to join together in married bliss, alongside directions to the local church.

But the rhyme could equally apply to maintaining a long-term romance with old-time traders. We need to find a way to preserve the best of the old even as we embrace the new – before it's too late.

It's not cheating to avail of the choices offered by supermarkets. Yet why must we abandon these once bustling little businesses in the process? We resemble magpies, with our fickle fondness for anything shiny and foreign. As if homespun stores with actual surnames on their signs are second-rate.

Resulting in 'something borrowed' becoming the burdensome reality for these retailers. Because once swamped by debts, longevity is no guarantee of survival.

Which leaves us all with 'something blue', in the form of towns devoid of charm and character, having allowed these cornerstones of the community go under.

So I was reminded by a sad little snippet in a local newspaper, concerning the closure of one of the oldest shops in another area. What made its demise all the more depressing was the fact that it had been in business for 99 years. Yet they didn't get to mark their centenary.

Some say we have a duty to support local shops. But shouldn't doing so be a delight? Or do we really want to surround ourselves with soulless shopping malls and chain stores, their head offices located on far-flung continents?

And it's not just locals who lose out because of a lack of loyalty. Many visit these shores in search of independent stores that have vanished from their own communities.

The owner of the 150-year-old clothes shop on this town's Main Street has kept the original name above her door. Which is how tourists from New Zealand were able to sit at the very same desk where their father had once worked as a tailor decades before, in what turned out to be 'a very tearful encounter'.

The proprietor cuts to the chase – as you might expect from someone with a propensity for plastering the walls with sassy posters. Including a 'bullshit bag' that catches my eye while she was talking.

'They were very emotional just coming in here, because so little has changed. The tourists want the shops with old names, Fiona – but they are disappearing. The planners give all the space to the Aldis and Tescos – when these are the places that are unique to Ireland.'

Because you know what they also say? If it ain't broke – don't fix it.

And definitely forget divorce.

Savour a season of swift change over coffee

Whatever about the journey that led me to this lovely country town, probably the most talked about travels of all time are those of a certain Lemuel Gulliver that were published on this day *(28 October)* in 1726. Just eight years short of three centuries, *Gulliver's Travels* has never been out of print.

This part novel, part adventure, part prose satire is often categorized as a children's book, yet adults also adore it. That giant of 20th-century literature and political prophet, George Orwell, confessed that he read it repeatedly and would put it on any list of 'six books which were to be preserved when all others were destroyed'.

Though it's not just today but this colourful time of year in general that is infused with Swift's spirit, given he was born on November 30, 1667 and died on October 19, 1745. He was aptly autumnal and even wintry in ways, with even those who knew him best baffled by his contradictions. One friend described his character as 'exceedingly strange, various and perplexed'.

For Swift was both a free spirit yet fiercely loyal to those he loved. He sought financial security yet shunned fame and even sabotaged success. Certainly, *Gulliver's Travels* was published anonymously, while his pamphlets made him powerful enemies who could block potential appointments.

Both his genius and supposed misanthropy surely stem from his bizarre upbringing. It is debatable that the man who died seven months before Swift was born was his real father.

Even stranger, Swift's wet nurse abducted him when he was a baby and took him to England, yet his family did not object. Indeed, his mother promptly moved to England when he was finally brought back to Dublin.

Stella was undoubtedly the love of his life, beside whom he is buried. But Swift was also close to another much younger woman, Esther Vanhomrigh. He may not have offered her commitment, but his term of endearment for her gave the world the beautiful name of Vanessa.

The secret lovers communicated mostly by letter, using the world 'coffee' as code for copulation. Rendering their correspondence comically risqué: 'I wish I were to walk with you 50 times about your garden, and then drink your coffee,' goes one steamy snippet.

'I drank no coffee since I left you . . . there is none worth drinking but yours,' swoons another.

At one point, the absence of this seriously stimulating drink interferes with Swift's work: 'I am not cheerful enough to write, for I believe coffee once a week is necessary to do that.'

Making me suspect that Swift might stay put if he travelled through time to this country town.

Because with so many cafes serving coffee, love wouldn't be short and sweet so much as swift yet sure to last.

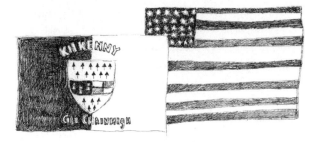

The brave ballad of James McHale

Joe tells me that he had to cut down his hundred-year-old apple trees, after big storms knocked them about. But hopefully, he adds, in a year or two they will grow back.

It seems an appropriate answer, given that we are part of a gathering to bid farewell to James McHale. This actor and poet who hailed from Hell's Kitchen, New York, ended his days amid the loving support of his many friends around this country town that he long called home.

But rallying around those in their hour of need is what we do so well. The Maria Keating Foundation meant that James was able to keep warm, without heating bills to add to the phenomenal woes of his last winter.

His funeral service took place in the Kingsriver Community, where he spent his final weeks.

The centre provides residential and day-care programmes for adults and young people with special needs. But thanks to James's close friends, it extended its embrace to include this man whose days had been so starkly numbered.

He lived here in a mobile home, Tibetan prayer flags blowing in the breeze on decking that looks out over fields, trees, and an old stone bridge. The same one where his hearse paused after the humanist service, so mourners could cast flowers into the river.

They watched them float away, as James had done, going onwards in their journey. The next chapter of which has got to be better for all like him who are faced with a terminal illness.

Katie, who works in O'Keeffe's, had tears in her eyes as she recalled never once since his diagnosis hearing him complain. Though James was no quiet American.

'Who is that guy?' strangers would ask about the tall figure cutting a dash about town. Known variously as 'the Yank', 'the pirate', even 'Excalibur', he was loud and full of life.

Maybe loss is more keenly felt in small communities, where we form part of each other's landscape. On my way home, I passed a house opposite the one where James lived, as usual flying the county colours. But that day an American flag wavered beside it. While white ribbons were tied around pillars outside his former landlord's home.

A friend read excerpts from one of his journals. Gems like 'Cupid's arrow sometimes lands in the crotch.' 'I've broken many hearts — mostly my own' had a poignant twist.

'You must strive to love life,' he wrote, 'even if it doesn't always love you.' 'Every day is a fresh canvas; every breath a brush.' And 'if you have hell to pay, best not ask for an itemised bill.'

He followed his own advice that when 'eventually death comes calling — make it crawl.'

While in another quip worthy of Oscar Wilde, he reckoned 'a good eulogy is worth dying for.'

Maybe so. But we'll miss such sound bites from this beloved blow-in from 'the big apple'.

Jill's cows are in paradise, not on the dinner plate

Autumn is full of colourful contradiction. For though this season announces the year's approaching retirement, it can hardly be said to be the retiring type. Certainly, the trees around this country town are a riot of copper, gold and russet – fallen leaves stretching a stunning carpet over the earth.

Maybe that's a hint to us humans not to lose our mojo as we mature.

'If you feel like retiring – or if your health means you have to – that's fine. But sometimes you see people in their 60s onwards and still looking young, who are just hanging around, like they don't know what to do.'

So says Jill Smith, the farmer who created a sensation by retiring her herd after decades of hard graft in the dairy. Thanks to a gofundme campaign and the support of animal rescuers, some of the herd have already gone to the animal sanctuary in England. Another lorryload leaves before Christmas, with the rest going over the next 12 months.

Jill is blown away by the love that was shown to her bovines.

'I never thought people would give money to rescue cows,' she marvels. 'Maybe for cats and dogs – but in this country, cows are for the dinner plate. It's just unheard of. It's so brilliant.'

Her low expectations lay behind the decision to remain anonymous for so long.

'I didn't think it would kick off, so I wanted to keep it quiet for as long as I could, though I felt guilty about not telling people. But it was all so new to me in the beginning. Only for Charlie's Equine Rescue [the centre which organized the campaign], I don't know what I'd have done.'

And while this 70-year-old plans to take life a little easier, she has no intention of being idle. Some of the very old cows that were not fit to travel will spend the rest of their days on the farm – 'to keep me occupied and sane,' says Jill. 'As my mother said, you want to die with the buckets in your hand.'

This lively expression was inspired by Jill's aunt May. 'She was out feeding the dogs – she always had cocker spaniels, for generations – when she dropped dead at the door. 'T'was lovely,' Jill says, in that quintessentially Irish way. 'Of course, her family were in shock – but what a way to go. A bucket in each hand and in her work clothes, with her wellies on.'

But though Jill is keeping a firm hold of her buckets, she is finally starting to relax after the bedlam involved in making bovine history.

'There were so many things to pull together, so much to do beforehand to make it happen. It's hard to believe they are actually over there.'

Jill admits that she pines for her beloved bovines.

'I miss their faces around the yard. There isn't a night goes by that I don't dream about the cattle.' While the cows probably miss their fair-minded farmer too, they are undoubtedly over the moo(n).

For they say that if you love someone, you should set them free.

And their human pal showed her true colours by giving them freedom – instead of fear – as their finale.

Time stands still as minority enjoy savage season

Much has changed since I moved to the country; from floods to financial droughts. But time seems to stand still when it comes to certain aspects of rural life, as I'm reminded on this last Sunday in September.

I'm referring not to the cycle of seasons, but tradition.

For while we have happily rid ourselves of many century-old customs, the defining aspect of the remaining ones is that they are blood sports that hurt vulnerable animals for the profit and pleasure of a minority, who nevertheless demand that they are preserved and paid for by the rest of us.

And they are: The Irish Greyhound Board will reportedly receive over €14m of taxpayers' money this year *(2016)* – an increase of over €1m on the previous year.

Despite a recent statement from the Greyhound Owners and Breeders Federation, which represents those involved in greyhound racing and hare coursing, which suggested the industry has rising debts and plummeting attendance and sponsorship.

Yet all over Ireland right now, hares are being held in cages so that these wild creatures can be turned into the hare-coursing equivalent of circus animals, as they are 'trained' to run around wire-enclosed fields with giant dogs in savage pursuit. For yet another nearly six-month long coursing season will be under way before next week's *Sunday Independent* is in your hands.

As always, some hares will be maimed or killed. Others will die from trauma and injuries after their release.

Which was probably what happened to the hare that I found at the side of a country road last year, the only one that I have seen in all my years here.

The beautiful creature was not yet decomposed, though a few ugly flies were hovering.

Spain and Portugal are the only other countries in the world where hare coursing is still legal.

The parallels are interesting. Just as the rights of a minority to have its idea of fun matter more than the protection due the endangered Irish hare, so too do Spain's animal welfare laws allow animals to be mistreated for the benefit of blood fiestas.

And though the latest polls suggest that over 70% of Spanish citizens oppose bullfighting – with thousands taking to the streets of Madrid earlier this month to demand an end to this centuries-old tradition – those in power support this blood sport of a small but influential group.

As reflected by the Portuguese President of the European Commission, Jose Manuel Barroso, who overturned Portugal's 76-year-old ban on 'death bullfighting' when he was the country's prime minister.

While back home, our Government – along with all the major political parties – denied us the democratic right last summer to decide whether to ban hare coursing.

Perhaps proving that power is itself a perverse pleasure – which sadly is with us for all time.

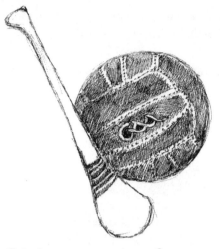

GAA sports of steaks versus sandwiches

As a former city slicker, I may know nothing much about GAA. But I can certainly see that people around these parts go gaga over hurling. Kids carry hurleys the way some city nippers nurse mobile phones.

And it's not just the boys; my neighbour, Ger Walsh, gave out yards to me last year when I wrote about hurling but failed to mention camogie. He says the girls are arguably more disciplined and dedicated players.

Of course, the county is currently on a humongous high after their latest win. But passing the well-tended statue of legendary local hurler, Ollie Walsh, the other evening, I wondered if the county had the same *grá* for Gaelic football. So I asked Ger's brother, Martin, its literal state of play here.

'Non existent,' he answered, without hesitation. 'It's all hurling. Hurling is a religion in Kilkenny. End of.'

Then he paused. 'Well, actually, we were Senior Club Football champions five times. Myself and Ger played, and I captained the Kilkenny team.'

Back then, football used to kick in when the hurling season finished. 'Ollie Walsh trained us to play football as well. We won the Intermediate County Final in hurling in 1983, the same year we won a Football Senior. I have five Senior Football Cup medals. If I was in Kerry, I'd be famous!'

And there's the rub. For it seems Gaelic football was unfairly treated in this county.

'I remember at the time, back in the eighties,' Martin says, 'we were training with the Kilkenny hurling team on frosty February nights. We'd all be in the same dressing rooms; the hurlers would be running up and down with us. But when it was time to get a feed afterwards, the guy standing at the restaurant door would ask: "hurler or footballer? Hurler — that way! Footballer — that way!" They were getting steaks, while we were eating sandwiches!'

But he remembers 'great times' playing the game. And the tradition still goes on; his young fellow played with the under-14s two years ago, when the Feile was in Derry.

'They were beaten by a team from New York. It's a brilliant way of people meeting each other.'

The dual dynamic still exists in some counties.

'In Clare this year, there is one club, Cratloe, which is in both the Senior Football and Senior Hurling. The same guys are playing for both. And they're just from small villages; they might have 20 players in total.'

Then Martin says something that encapsulates our native, if sometimes nutty, genius. He tells me that playing Gaelic football and hurling involve 'completely different skills, but it's basically the same Irish kind of thing.'

Which is?

'Ah, you know. Just kind of tearing into each other.' He smiles. 'You don't get that in soccer.'

Learning the hard way how to be kind

Summer — when the living is supposedly easy — is well and truly over for the children in this country town, who are once more busy learning. But even if oversized bags weigh them down, at least getting thrashed by teachers doesn't feature on the timetable.

For such was the experience of education that many of their grandparents endured, back when teachers in this county were issued a leather strap, bamboo shoot or a ruler, along with some chalk and a duster.

As one local remembers: 'It was common for pupils to leave school at the end of the day with bleeding hands or split lips.'

Some teachers turned their backs on these perverse tools of pedagogy — but only because they favoured using their fists.

Not knowing when a teacher would literally lash out added to the terror. 'They slapped you for anything or for nothing. Some days were worse than others.'

While the uncomfortable truth is that those who should have cherished children the most often colluded in the cruelty.

'You never mentioned the slaps at home or your parents would give you another few, and maybe worse ones, for good measure.'

Nor was it only religious orders that behaved in this ungodly fashion. Plenty of lay teachers vented their frustrations.

Such as the teacher who quit smoking for Lent and 'flung a bundle of books at us with all his might. Then he picked up a leather with one hand and a bamboo rod with the other, and he ran down between the desks, striking to the right and to the left like a cavalryman at the Charge of the Light Brigade'.

The so-called fair sex could be just as ferocious. One national school teacher in the 1940s used to 'tear around the classroom with a shoe in her hand, hopping sometimes to avoid getting a splinter from the floorboards. She'd hit us on the head, the hands, the shoulders – anywhere she could reach. By God, did it hurt. Many of us were covered in heel marks from that shoe'.

A sick sense of humour sometimes accompanied the abuse. Like the teacher who hanged a boy from an iron hanger on the classroom wall, close to a large crucifix, and left him dangling by his braces for a quarter of an hour.

When he finally went to take him down, the teacher turned to the class and jibed: 'Well now, lads, was he the good thief or the bad thief, what do ye think?'

Of course, he didn't expect a reply. Though probably those children would have been too traumatised to articulate one, if their sensibilities weren't already blunted by the brutality.

But hopefully they saw that a bad thief was asking the question, for he was robbing them of both their innocence and confidence.

Realising that would have restored some of the latter. And if the former was forever gone, at least it was replaced by the determination to be decent to anyone as vulnerable as they once were.

Then the school of hard knocks would have taught them a valuable life lesson.

Inconvenient truth of horse-racing cast-offs

Horse trailers regularly pass through this country town, en route to the nearby racing track. For, as Europe's largest producer of thoroughbreds, isn't it always the season in Ireland?

And the Government plans to make the industry even bigger, recently *(2015)* increasing its budget to Irish horse racing from €43m to €54.5m, with pledges of further increases over the coming years.

'This is an investment,' said Minister Coveney, citing how the industry is worth over a billion euro a year and provides employment to over 15,000 people.

Certainly, Coveney knows the business is booming. So much so that his Department of Agriculture has had to increase the number of licensed horse slaughter plants from just one in 2008 to more than five, to cope with demand.

For, as John Joe Fitzpatrick from Shannonside Foods in Straffan has pointed out, 80% of the 2,200 horses slaughtered at his purpose-built plant last year were thoroughbreds. And 60% of them would have raced.

The horses are sent for disposal for numerous reasons – poor track performance, career-ending injuries, and temperament issues. According to Fitzpatrick, the factory is the cheapest way to dispose of a horse.

But spare a thought for those who cannot profit from their 'useless' horses, as United Farmers Association President Bernie Wall calls them, thanks to the 'unfit for human consumption' stamp on many horse passports.

'I'm sure the owners are quite distressed to do this for their animals,' Wall added.

Which is debatable, judging by the number of slaughter trucks stuffed to the gills with last season's stud farm cast-offs that routinely pass my window. Many even have livestock trailers attached, where you can see the horses within, often with bits and bridles.

One particular vehicle caught my eye last summer. Not because it was so ugly; all cold steel, with only one thin slat three-quarters way up the side providing air on that stultifying hot day. No, it was the fact that the driver and his female passenger were dressed in casual equestrian gear.

I spotted the vehicle at a gas station a little later. There was no sign of the driver and his passenger. But the horses were still locked in that mean-spirited truck, because they were shaking it from side to side.

Eventually the driver and passenger emerged from the shop, licking on 99s. They got in and drove off with their cargo of useless horses.

It adds pathos to the legend 'Caution Horses', which is often emblazoned on those other equine carriers. For it could be read as a warning to horses that don't make the grade.

Because with Horse Racing Ireland's Joe Keeling's plan to use some of the increased government funding to give the Curragh a face-lift, you won't win any bets for guessing who will continue to pay the price for those who always make a profit.

WINTER

We'll be in deep water unless we see sense

The floods have me thinking about the previous occupants of this country town cottage; two bachelor boyos who experienced the biblical phrase 'my cup runneth over' all too literally this month back in 1947, when the river burst its banks and washed their afternoon tea away.

Now it's beginning to look possible to step into the same river twice. Or rather, to have it step in here for a second time. Maybe what happened back then isn't so much water under the bridge, as a soon to be released soggy sequel.

Though the local butcher says this street is always the last in town to flood. But with the weather going haywire on and off for months, I'm taking nothing for granted. Especially as normally it's just the river bank beneath the backyard that disappears. The strip of grass above it, which I optimistically call 'the garden', remains dry.

But the entire lot was submerged last week. My Deputy Dawg kept looking through the gate, wondering where all the green stuff had gone.

He's not the only one, as the other 'green stuff' has long since disappeared for those many unfortunate homeowners and traders who are drowning in debt, thanks to repeated flooding. With no insurance coverage, how are they supposed to stay afloat?

The butcher's premises lies in the flood firing line too, a mark at the top of his back door indicating how high the water rose in 1947. Another reminder is the huge slab of wood on the counter upon which he chops up carcasses. It was found washed up that year.

Clearly, the flood taketh as well as giveth. There were no panes of glass in those days, only shutters, and the slab floated out the butcher's window during another deluge that devastating February. They were lucky to retrieve it and have held on to it since.

But I don't blame rivers for bursting their banks, what with all the toxic fertilisers and animal waste we keep pumping into them. After all, rivers are a symbol of life. And perhaps life is fed up with this one frail form of it arrogantly behaving as if it has the right to meddle with the rest of life on this planet.

Let's hope we come down to earth soon. Because if we continue getting swept away by our own importance, we may lose our footing on terra firma forever.

Wintery ways reveal our heart of darkness

Leaves may still linger on some trees, but their top branches are usually bare. While the colours have become coppery and brittle. Nor does it take a breeze, let alone a wind, to send them falling any more. Winter and its ever-encroaching darkness is upon us.

The clock going back didn't help. Some question if this custom is now a cynical commercial ruse to lure us into lit-up Christmas shops.

Regardless of fleeting light, the farmers are busy. Tractors trundle over the bridge from dawn to dusk in this country town. Some are still hauling in hay and other produce. You often hear before you see the mammoth machinery.

They may be impressive, but my favourite farming vehicle is an old tractor that used to be parked everywhere about town, as if it was a car. Certainly, it was small and dinky enough to fit into tight spaces.

That tractor is viewed as a comical curiosity. Yet only a few decades ago, it would have been the last word in technical wizardry. Because hard as it is to fathom, with our SUVs and science fiction savvy, farmers once relied on horse power instead of high tech.

As did the rest of society. Indeed it was as late as this day 47 years ago *(15th November 1968)*, that our national public transport providers at CIE retired its last dray horses.

These are the largest of the horse breeds, which were bred for tough tasks, like pulling heavy loads and ploughing. Dray horses are extremely muscular and strong. They also possess a natural curiosity and willingness to learn, as well as a docile demeanour.

It's no wonder that you regularly see them in equestrian centres, where their calm and sweet-tempered personality makes them ideal for nervous or inexperienced riders.

So it was hard to hear a local remembering the time as a boy when he witnessed these gentle giants being led over the bridge, in a trail as endless as today's tractors, by the farmers they had worked so hard and willingly for their entire lives. For technology, in the form of the new-fangled tractors, had arrived.

Their last journey was to the old watchtower that stands on the far side of the bridge. That ancient castle has been the site of strange and savage scenes over the centuries, not least when it was used during that time as an abattoir. Toothed eels thrived on the blood and guts that were dumped into the river.

Those trusting creatures were brought there at the end of their final working day. That local boy, now a man, remembers the struggles that took place, when those extraordinarily powerful equines realized their fate. For this was also before more sophisticated forms of slaughter had been perfected.

Under cover of night, we brutally extinguished their light as thanks for their labour.

Thereby expanding our all too human heart of darkness.

Festive spirit is a gift that cannot be bought

County Kilkenny is the place to be at Christmas, firstly because its many stables remind you of the Christian saviour's humble origins. Surely no mistake, since He preached that the Kingdom of Heaven lies within, not in material wealth.

So it's ironic that we honour His birthday with an orgy of consumerism and commercialism. Buying presents isn't enough: visiting Santa is essential. You pay a sizeable entrance fee into glitzy grottos so your children can enjoy the ultimate experience.

It was less sophisticated when I was a child. Our local grotto was constructed mostly of crepe paper, while the man himself bore little resemblance to the one on the 'Lemons' Sweets box. The grotto in Switzer's on Grafton Street was considered the real thing.

Speaking of 'the real thing', Santa's outfit was a fabrication of the Coca Cola Company, to encourage us to equate happiness with its product.

But hold the 'bah humbug', for Santa was inspired by a real human being, the philanthropist Saint Nicholas, who lived during the fourth century.

Amazingly, the saint's resting place is in nearby Jerpoint Park. His remains are thought to have been moved here by early crusaders, 800 years ago.

But Thomastown boasts the ultimate festive 'Celebrity in Residence', for Santa Claus's headquarters is located on Market Street.

Both young and old are free to peer through the window and feast their eyes on his cosy home. His rocking chair is set before a table, where a pair of reading glasses lie across an open atlas.

Changes occur daily; his fire-side slippers are replaced by a hefty pair of Wellington boots. A blackboard calendar chalks the countdown to Christmas, while a growing list of children's names scrolls across the floor.

The success of this wonderland lies in one priceless ingredient: the generosity of spirit of the O'Neill family who created it. This is the second year that they've given the town a magical glimpse into Father Christmas's home.

They've little to gain from it, business-wise. Their shop a few doors up is no threat to the Goliaths of the surrounding supermarkets and shopping centres.

Most magically, they've made it believable that Santa Claus has his headquarters in the modest heart of a country town.

For surely a famously jolly man, inspired by a saviour who was born in a manger and rejected worldly possessions, would never base himself among those with big budgets for professional designers with strategies to make us spend more.

Wouldn't he be more likely to choose as neighbours a close-knit family with a great sense of fun? Thereby reminding us that people of good cheer exist right under our Rudolph-red noses, all year round.

That's a true Christmas message.

The tragic twist to a squandered second chance

The last of the leaves fall to the earth to lie like wasted gold coins beneath the gable end of a stone wall facing a quiet country road – though it was once the main route between Graiguenamanagh and this town. A plaque mounted on it 20 years ago this month *(November 1998)* remembers when it was the thriving forge of Henry Hammond.

Little is known of this lost hero of 1798, whose ancestors were blacksmiths who came to Ireland as part of the Norman invasion and settled in the area. Presumably his profession meant he was physically strong. It also bestowed privileges, such as the freedom to travel to other forges and to the estates of the aristocracy.

Some say Hammond was a captain in the United Irishmen Forces. Certainly, he was well placed to collect and pass on information.

And it was the smiths who armed the rebels. For the uprising was born of a bloody era, when violence was used to force change, inspired by the mob might of the French revolution. Few would have supported Daniel O'Connell's famous dictum: 'No cause is worth the shedding of a single drop of human blood.'

Buckets of which soaked the earth during the Battle of New Ross that June. Hammond was present at the Rower camp, leading to his arrest soon after. He was tried at Kilkenny for making pikes and sentenced to death by hanging.

But if Hammond's life hung by a thread, he was unbelievably blessed that it was well connected. For aristocrats had the power in those days to grant freedom to three condemned people each year. Miss Eleanor Doyle's intervention led to Hammond's release.

That should be the 'all's well that ends well' of Hammond's happily ever after.

One version of events has family and friends waiting at the prison gates to take him home. The other sees Hammond walking miles by himself.

Both scenarios find him entering Murphy's pub in this country town.

It's easy to imagine that relief at cheating death brought on a raging thirst. Only Hammond didn't stop at a few drinks. By all accounts, he went on an almighty bender that lasted the evening, singing rebel songs and making derogatory remarks about the redcoats. Many of who were raw after one of the bloodiest battles of the rebellion, and deeply resentful of Hammond's release.

Word got out and Hammond was rearrested and brought back to jail in Kilkenny. This time there was no reprieve.

Less than 24 hours after his second chance, Hammond was publicly hung, drawn and quartered. His home was burned to the ground and the forge never again used for its original purpose. It is said members of the Hammond family were deported or else fled after his execution.

For bright sparks may fly but they still die out, extinguished where they land.

And even a miracle didn't hammer home the point to the brave but foolhardy Hammond to lay down the hammer and just be glad he could go home.

Why saying hello can make us fare well in life

It's said that we talk about the weather so much not just because a day can start off dull and overcast, yet by noon the sun is sparkling on the river in this country town.

For we are almost unique as a people in wanting to give each other the time of day, quite literally, in words or a smile or nod.

We can take for granted that Ireland is one of the few places in the world where people greet each other when they pass – even though this is arguably the epitome of courtesy and civilised behaviour, as well as the most optimistic of overtures. For we have such faith in the saying that 'strangers are friends not yet met', that we put it into action, whenever we encounter them.

It is also an invaluable way to protect the most vulnerable among us. For acknowledging someone tells them that we see them, even if they feel invisible because of private woes.

The simple, yet stunning act of hailing another human being, can prevent them from retreating into reclusive isolation and depression – keeping them afloat long enough to hopefully start to swim instead of sinking ever deeper into despair.

But then, I've always been a fan of saying 'hello' to all and sundry – whether they like it or not, even as a child growing up in the city. Though I rein it in when I visit 'the Big Smoke' these days, as many people would react with suspicion or even fear if you greeted them. However, city folk are friendly, once there's an icebreaker to enable conversation.

Greeting strangers is still the norm in rural Ireland, though some country folk can blank you. I have learned not to bother with those who look the other way or even scowl if you smile at them, for nobody enjoys being snubbed.

Contrary to expectations, often they are older folk, for many kids mumble a greeting or shyly smile.

While I always acknowledge a neighbour who also acknowledges me, even though we vehemently disagree on blood sports. I am grateful for our mutual good manners that prompt us to make the effort.

'Even if you don't see eye to eye, it's good to keep talking because you never know when you might need each other,' a store owner in this country town says.

I admire his pragmatism, for many of us take our petty grievances, prejudices or ourselves too seriously.

'If you don't sort it out,' he adds, 'the grievance can go on – even for generations.'

'So few people say "hello" to each other any more,' laments a local who lost heart after a recent brief, but bleak, encounter.

She heard someone on the radio say that one New Year resolution we should all make is to say 'hello' to everyone we pass. She had taken it on board – only for two women who she greeted to ignore her,

While increasingly, some folk don't see you because they're too busy staring at their smart phones.

'Will the word "hello" disappear from our language?' she wonders.

Not as long as such friendly folk continue to flourish, come rain or shine.

When all seems lost, heaven can still be found

The claps of thunder were so loud one recent night that I thought a lorry had crashed into the house across the road – again – until lightning lit up the river just beyond our yard.

At one point, it rose so high that I feared it might run off with 'River Run'. It did in 1947, washing away the lean-to. The floods that year were accompanied by a financial outlook as bleak as today's, as my father reminded me, with a story about that fearsome February and a £5 note.

He was a young boy growing up in Co Offaly that spring, which saw the worst weather in Ireland in 40 years. Poverty exposes you to the brunt of the elements, as he learnt. His father was a heavy gambler, particularly on greyhounds running for the Waterloo Cup, and lacking a winning streak. His big butchering business was ruined by 1940, thanks to falling cattle prices.

But that February, my father's mother had a £5 note, an astronomical sum of money when you consider that the price of an average house was £400. It was a gift from her uncle, John, then parish priest of Dunboyne. He kept an eye on his delicate niece, who had been disowned for marrying a dreamy-eyed man twice her age.

So my father set off with his mother on the two-mile walk from their rented home in Ballycrystal to the village of Geashill, a veritable Manhattan of the midlands, with its pubs and shops.

I can imagine their excitement, after weeks of low-lying hunger, at the prospect of all the provisions that precious paper would buy.

They passed the Laceys, who were big horse people, and the Donaldsons, where everyone went for sporting events because they owned the only radio for miles.

It wasn't until they reached 'Bun' Dunnes' house (so-called because he was just five foot tall) that his mother realised that she had lost the note.

Shaking with devastation, she rechecked her pockets in vain. There was nothing for it but to walk back the mile they'd come, looking for a faded piece of paper in the falling snow.

Where the thought of treats to come had warmed them, now the wind blew bitter through thin coats. It was easy to keep their eyes trained on the ground, for that was where their hearts lay.

And then – against all odds – they found the £5 note.

My father said it was like they'd gone to heaven when they saw it, lying in a pothole.

It's over six decades since that day, but my father swears he could still drive to the exact spot on the byroad.

So keep your eyes open, if you can't keep your chin up. And even if spring isn't in the air, it might find its way into your step.

I had to wing it when a visitor surprised me

The less than crafty crows that raid my bird table give the game away by making a squawky song and dance about it. Their even more colossal cousins, the rooks, perch like sooty sentinels on the railings of the nearby bridge. They aren't interested in such small fry as bird seed.

So I was taken aback to see one in the backyard last winter solstice. I went to shoo him, but realised that he was injured. Huge and unwieldy, he literally backed himself into a corner. Blood was spilling from a cut in his leg.

'It's OK,' I told him, without conviction.

'Call yourself a rook whisperer?' his black eyes looked back at me, bright with intelligence and awareness of the terrible state he was in.

He pecked pathetically at the bird food I threw his way; grasping at seeds in the absence of straws.

I fenced off the area, so my 'Deputy Dawg' couldn't harm him, and padded a cardboard box with stuffing from an old cushion.

Then I dropped by Lisa, a veterinary nurse who runs a dog-grooming parlour.

'Cat food,' she said, holding shears in one hand and a half-shorn Shih Tzu by the other.

At first the rook backed away when I stepped close, but soon he relaxed. He enthusiastically plunged his beak into the cat food, till it resembled a skewer of lamb kebab.

But the sky was darkening: the shortest day of the year was drawing rapidly to a close. As too, I feared, was the life of this wild creature. For the rook stopped eating and drinking as evening fell. He stood facing the wall, huddled under a makeshift roof I had fashioned.

I placed slates next to him, along with a hot water bottle. I thought of him during that long winter's night, wind howling and rain falling relentlessly. I was afraid of what the following day would bring.

But to my delight, I found the resilient rook busily limping around his new residence, pecking at his bowls and perky with purpose. At some point during the night, he had taken stuffing from the cardboard box and placed it next to the slates that shielded him.

I went out to gather twigs and dry moss to make him a better bed. But when I returned, the rook was gone.

Something caught my eye and I looked up to see him standing on the wall. Then he lifted off, circling the yard twice before disappearing from view.

Maybe it was a slight case of 'empty nest syndrome' that led me to still put the moss and twigs in the cardboard box in case he returned. He never did.

But sometimes I see a rook hovering nearby. And I remember the time I took one under my wing.

Scapegoats and dark secrets in a small Irish town

Posters for various events are displayed around this country town, vying for the attention of passers-by. One that caught my eye recently was a play called *Lovers Meeting*. For the lack of an apostrophe brought to mind the infamous case of Mary 'Moll' McCarthy, the mother of seven children by, it's said, as many different men, whose murder this month back in 1940 remains unsolved.

The twists and turns of this horrible whodunit seems endless, what with the killer's identity supposedly an open secret among the community at the time, and suspects that included a priest and local gardaí.

The IRA was also embroiled. Indeed, some claim this is why their former chief, Sean McBride, failed in his defence of Henry 'Harry' Gleeson. Leading to this innocent man being executed for the crime.

Gleeson received the first posthumous pardon in the history of this State only two years ago (*in 2015*). Little wonder this not so ancient history still haunts locals, like the woman who lives a short distance from Marlhill, near New Inn, County Tipperary, where the murder occurred. She always thinks of Harry Gleeson whenever she sees a neighbour walking his greyhounds – for Gleeson loved his greyhounds too.

Maybe the bachelor was right to favour canine company, given his treatment at human hands in a town where – like Moll McCarthy, who was used and abused by so many of its men — he was a blow-in.

Certainly, Moll's killer guessed correctly that Gleeson (who worked on his uncle's farm next door to Moll) would be the one to find her lying dead in one of the fields, that wintry morning of November 21, with two gunshots wounds to her face.

And that then – prompted by civic duty and the dangerous lack of guile of the innocent – he would walk into the trap by calling to the guards to report his grim discovery.

Though how Moll survived as long as she did is itself a miracle.

She had already riled the other women in the village by naming her sons after their already married fathers, and her daughters after the fathers' mothers.

The women retaliated by repeatedly bringing Moll to court, hoping in the process to get rid of those living reminders of their husbands' infidelity, some of whom likely resembled their own children. But Judge Troy would not condemn her.

Their problem was solved when someone got rid of Moll forever. Making it finally possible to visit the sins of the fathers upon her brood, who were sent away and never heard of again.

Until decades later, when an elderly lady grew weepy one night and confided her lamentable life story in a friendly nurse. She explained how she had been locked up in an institution after she witnessed her mother's murder in their home. Before her body was dumped in a field, where another unmarried soul was doomed to discover it.

Harry Gleeson's pardon was announced on April 1 – widely known as April Fools' Day.

Which adds a tragic twist to the expression 'fool for love'.

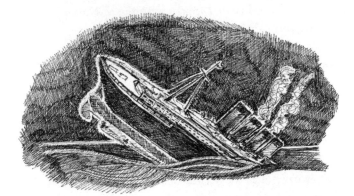

Good souls are neither saints nor sinners

Today's All Saints Day is spiritually sandwiched between the spooky high jinks of Halloween and All Souls Day. The latter shifts the focus from the saintly to the rest of us sinners, who must pass through purgatory before we are pure enough for heaven.

But many question the existence of this intermediate state. As one philosopher said: 'Life can only be understood backwards; but it must be lived forward.'

Yet rarely is the experience black and white.

So I was reminded, ironically, by 60 black and white images from the Poole Lusitania collection in Cobh, Co Cork, marking the 100th anniversary of the infamous sinking of that passenger ship (*in 1915*).

What struck me was how haunted the survivors appeared. Most looked lost instead of lucky.

Like Captain Turner. The gold braid of his uniform saved him, when a sailor saw its glint after he had been in the water for three hours.

Yet Turner looks in turmoil, hurrying along with his head down. Did he torture himself with the belief that a captain should go down with his ship?

Or was he remembering the warnings that were issued before the *Lusitania* set sail? They caused ripples of unease, but were chalked up to wartime intimidation. Turner reportedly called it 'the best joke I've heard in days'.

Surely all struggled with the randomness of life's lottery. Which might explain the uneasy expressions of parents Annie and Edward Riley and their two children, Ethel and Sutcliffe. Apparently they were the only full family to survive the tragedy intact. In contrast to orphaned Helen Smith, aged six, pictured with the US Consul. She was playing on deck, away from her parents, when the torpedo struck.

And there is a titanic difference between fiction and fact. The captioned image 'A shipboard romance' shows survivors Gerda Neilson and John Welsh. Gerda, a milliner, met and fell in love with mechanical engineer John during the voyage, who proposed marriage.

John kept Gerda afloat until they were rescued. They married soon after. However, Gerda was so traumatised by the tragedy that she went insane and lived in a mental hospital until her death in 1961.

Maybe we are saints and sinners simultaneously. Millionaire Alfred Gwynne Vanderbilt was in the dining saloon when disaster struck. Coming on deck, he encountered a woman and child who were without life jackets. Vanderbilt gave the panicked woman his belt, despite the fact that he could not swim. As the ship sank, he urged his valet to 'find all the kiddies you can'.

He was last seen at the railing as the ship went down, standing calmly with two elderly passengers whose fates were similarly sealed. His widow and three young sons survived him.

Vanderbilt's body was never found. But undoubtedly his soul was.

Goon but not Forgotten

'Tis the season to share wisdom of funnyman Spike

'Tis the season to be jolly,' so the chirpy carol goes. Making Christmas especially challenging for those with crosses to bear. A season celebrating a birth doesn't exactly help when burdened with bereavement — or if battling the blues.

Yet where is the spirituality behind the Christmas spirit to provide solace for such broken hearts? Shouldn't the Good News make bad times feel better? What can the gospel give Christians who grieve, beyond advising them to put their best foot forward in this vale of tears? Why can't light-heartedness accompany the way and the truth and the life?

So believed the 'funniest person of the last 1,000 years' as a BBC poll once voted Spike Milligan, who wrote how 'during this period when my faith was fading, I wished that somehow, somewhere, I'd come across something humorous – a comment or an incident – in my prayer book or Bible. Just one line like "And lo, Jesus laugheth heartily", or "Jesus sayeth 'Come unto me and I will tell you a joke'." But no such luck.'

He went on to say: 'Why? Why? I wonder. I suspect Christ peppered his teachings and parables with wit and repartee. He was a 'whole' man. And surely the message of religion is that we find happiness in it?'

For 'the great God of all' modern British comedy, as John Cleese hailed the born-in-India son of an Irish father and English mother, whose coffin was draped in the Irish flag, suffered with severe depression. So it seems fitting to remember him during this sometimes stressful season. Especially since the genius behind *The Goon Show* deeply respected Jesus.

'I still don't know what it's all about,' Milligan admitted, 'but all the world has to do is enact the teachings of Christ.'

Especially the ones practised by Saint Francis, in whose honour our current Pope is named. Indeed, Milligan wrote to Pope Paul VI in 1976, telling him that he had decided to withdraw from the Roman Catholic Church and become a Buddhist because he wouldn't excommunicate an American vivisectionist.

Milligan also once marched in to the Food Hall at Harrods and tried to stuff 28lb of spaghetti down the manager's throat, 'to give him some idea of how a goose feels being force-fed maize to make foie gras'.

Milligan's daughter, Laura, says her father's love of animals and life-long passion as an animal rights activist were born in India.

'He was incredibly sensitive and he witnessed terrible cruelty to animals by the soldiers over there.'

Fortunately for us, Milligan's coping strategy for his sadness was writing. One suitable seasonal poem that also encapsulates his convictions is *Rage In Heaven:*

If a robin redbreast in a cage
Puts all heaven in a rage
How feels heaven when
Dies the millionth battery hen?

Milligan's Jesus was not to be found pontificating from behind pearly gates, as reflected in his poignant poem, *Entertaining Angels Unawares:*

I thought I saw Jesus
On a tram
I said 'Are you Jesus?'
He replied 'Yes I am'.

Big blow-in is taking a gander around town

Some blow-ins to this country town are neither former city slickers nor folk from foreign shores, but our brother and sister creatures. Like the pigeon that arrived on a less than flying visit who has been strutting about the ramp of the bridge for what feels like forever.

Now a goose is giving town life a lash. There she was one morning, heralding her arrival by making an awful racket. The cawing crows and quacking ducks sound positively demure in contrast to this fog-horned fowl.

This incredible honk waddles about amicably with her mallard mates. Her black beak extends beyond her black eyes to a knob at the top of her head, as if someone wedged it there.

The gorgeous giant has beige and brown feathers, white stripes interwoven on the wings and front that match her stylish petticoat.

The goose is strong but hardly the silent type, so word soon got around, with locals coming down to the river to take a gander.

Cliches abounded over Christmas about whether this goose's goose would be cooked – just as pigeon pie jokes used to do the rounds. Fortunately, both survived the festive season.

But speculation was rife about the breed and background.

'She's from the Arctic,' said a local, in the authoritative tones of one who has spent years studying the approximately 30 species of geese on the globe.

Another believed it was a Brent goose – and hence a goner. For she had been land-bound so long that her wing muscles would be wasted.

'So she won't be able to take off,' the sage concluded sagely.

Other scaremongering swiftly followed. The goose was starving to death. For she was definitely getting thinner. The caring owner of a nearby business wondered what geese ate and hurried off to google their gourmet preferences.

Then there were savage tales that would give anyone goosebumps. *Jaws* didn't have a patch on this feathered fiend, because you didn't even have to step into the water for her to tear you limb by limb. Parents were warned to keep their kids away following gossip that the goose had bitten one.

Though some fearless folk continued to feed the famished fowl. One man even petted the chilling creature, the goose having the good manners not to maul him.

'She's lovely,' said a woman who regularly feeds the goose grub. 'I know it's silly, but she's got such kind eyes.'

Seems the woman might be right. Because contrary to popular misconception, geese not only form lifelong bonds with their feathered partners, but can be equally loving to the human who raises them.

This is especially true of this gentle girl, who turns out to be an African Goose, a domestic breed that is usually too heavy to fly.

Proving Mark Twain's adage that 'It ain't what you don't know that gets you into trouble. It's what you know for sure that ain't so'.

For all those theories about the tall stranger in town were on a wild goose chase.

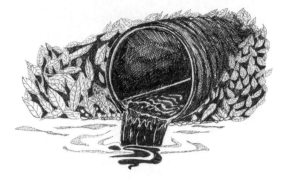

Wising up to the lack of fish in our salmon pool

Property developers have a penchant for calling their concrete creations after the natural wonders that were bulldozed to make way for them.

But not the salmon pool in this country town which lives up to its name, overlooking the stretch of river where this king of fish returns each year to spawn the next generation.

Though some would say you have as much chance of catching sight of this icon of Irish mythology as the heron hunched on the riverbank does of catching one for his dinner – for the Atlantic salmon population has declined drastically over the past 200 years. And the rate is accelerating, with average catches today some 80% lower than in the 1970s.

The survival rate of young salmon leaving our rivers has likewise plunged in that period with return rates of adults now as low as 5%.

Salmon Watch Ireland says man's destructive relationship with the natural world lies behind the many causes. These include climate change, pushing a drastically-altered environment at sea; technological advances in high seas fisheries; illegal fishing, and even the rise in wildlife predation, caused by the scarcity of traditional prey due to overfishing.

Inland Fisheries Ireland admitted last year (*2017*) that various conservation measures, including the decade-long ban on drift netting for salmon at sea, don't appear to have worked.

But perhaps there are elephants in the room that explain the scarcity of these fish in our waters – for there has been little focus on salmon farming, which has been practised in Ireland since the mid-1980s, with devastating consequences for both salmon and sea trout survival.

It is ironic that the industrialised farming of a fish renowned for instilling wisdom has not made us smarter.

But despite all the evidence, both the industry and successive governments continue to promote salmon farms – with some estimating a 78% rise in production by 2020.

Some opponents cite land-based farms as a possible compromise – which introduces the second elephant, that of the lethal link between what we put on our land and its effects on the water.

Along with acidic flushes through the degradation of peatlands and coniferous industry, intensive farming is ruining our rivers.

Environmentalists claim there is little or no management of river habitat or water-quality issues. River Trusts would seem to lack statutory powers and the full-time staff needed to be truly effective.

But it's not too late.

We could still save our salmon by laying off at least some of the land, designating certain areas as legally-protected habitat and allowing re-wilding to occur.

Otherwise, we face a chilling future, in which our country's children grow up thinking a salmon pool is just a nice name for an area, rather than a living place of natural reality.

Cold Christmas of more than a missing postman

Times have changed. For Christmas Day in 1929 found married father-of-four Larry Griffin putting on his postman's outfit as usual, before cycling from his home in south-east Ireland to deliver mail to the surrounding areas.

Much like the glass of good cheer awaiting Santa with his sack of goodies, it was customary to offer the man with the mailbag a thank you tipple. Presumably Griffin wasn't the only postie to be a tad tipsy as a result.

Though that's when this *Father Ted*-type tale takes a tragic turn, with Griffin doomed to become the unenviable enigma in the case of the missing postman.

For a conspiracy of silence persisted in the village where he was last seen, despite over 20 people allegedly witnessing what happened. Exposing the tenuous esteem in which the Church was held, for all its control, as bishops begged their congregations in vain for information.

The case caused huge embarrassment for the government; the innocence and ideals of the Free State arguably eclipsed by a new era where rights trumped responsibility.

It shamed the fledgling Garda Síochána, founded only seven years previously, especially as guards were among those charged with Griffin's murder.

They included other pillars of the community, such as schoolteacher Thomas Cashin, who drove around the guards looking for Griffin's body in the same car that was used to dispose of it.

After Griffin dropped three half crowns in the pub, Ned Morrissey picked them up and used them to buy drinks. There was a scuffle, before Morrissey deliberately tripped Griffin up, causing him to fatally fall.

Then darkness descended. Or as Jim Fitzgerald's testimony chillingly put it 'nobody said anything about going for the priest or doctor'.

Because it would have ruined publican Patrick Whelan, while others like Master Cashin and Garda Dullea and Murphy would have lost their jobs.

So they hid Griffin's body, the 10 defendants cheering when the case collapsed and they were acquitted. Many of them went on to profit from libel actions.

There were losers. Like Fitzgerald, the State's only witness until he withdrew his testimony after repeated threats. The labourer could not find work in the area afterwards and moved to Galway, ending his life in a home for the elderly poor.

While there is a cruel irony in the postman's wife, Mary, who received letters from time to time telling her where his body was, though nothing came of any search.

For not just a postman went missing that Christmas; where was compassion?

Griffin's grandson says the loss devastated the family, who longed for answers. But above all, 'just to get hold of the body, so they could give him a Christian burial.'

It seems apt that drinking in pubs was forbidden on another day, aside from the one celebrating the birth of a saviour who brought peace and goodwill.

Which was Good Friday, when we crucified Him.

Ireland's creepy castles of spooky squatters

Fog travels down the river that runs behind my backyard like a murky monster. The usual creaks and groans of this country-town cottage are louder during wayward weather, amplifying the eerie sounds of someone padding around upstairs.

Not that there's anything particularly peculiar about hearing someone mooching around overhead – except it happens when nobody else is here.

The supernatural shenanigans don't stop there. The lights often dim or brighten for no apparent reason, while the electricity sometimes randomly cuts off at night.

It doesn't bother me – but it sure can give the heebie jeebies to visitors. I returned from a weekend away last winter, to find the dogsitter camped out on a couch in the sitting room. She was so spooked by the freaky footsteps that she wouldn't sleep in the upstairs guest room.

Maybe these ghostly goings-on have something to do with the 1,000-year-old tower that stands opposite this cottage?

Much folklore surrounds castles in Ireland. Legend has it that many were magically built in one night, using bullock's blood in the mortar for good measure.

Certainly, there are no shortages of supernatural stories connected to these ancient stone structures. It is said that the wails of the slaughtered garrison at Carrignacurra, near Inchigeela, may still be heard on stormy nights – the sort of tale that is repeated about many castles.

Other hauntings abound, some of a romantic nature. Ireland's very own Romeo and Juliet are apparently still in residence at Ross Castle, beside Lough Sheelin. The ghosts are those of two unhappy young lovers who got caught up in a feud between their families – the Nugents and the O'Reillys.

Sometimes the spirits are malicious minxes. Like Cathleen Clare, who lived at Ferns Castle and made a practice of enticing young men to visit. She then showed them to a bed which opened like a trapdoor, hurling them into a foul pit below.

This went on until one lucky lad escaped. The sadistic siren paid for her crimes, we are told, at the market cross in Wexford.

Meanwhile, the gentle ghost of poor Sibeal Lynch still wails near Pierce Ferriter's castle at the end of the Dingle Peninsula. Pierce had stolen his charming captive away from her people. They were happy together, until the day Pierce's infuriated in-laws surrounded the castle.

Pierce hid Sibeal out of harm's way – or so he thought – in a cave beside the sea. Only to find, when the danger was past, that she had been drowned by the rising tide.

Ballymoy Castle in Laois is swept by mysterious beings every Saturday; which could be handy if you don't fancy housework.

But unless you're quicker on your feet than the ones up my stairs, it might be best to avoid my haunted home.

Heartbreaking hunts haunt this harsh winter

A heron has been haunting the river in this country town all winter, often hunting on the bank below my backyard. As I discover when I step outside. For he spreads his huge, slate-grey wings and flaps ponderously away.

I feel bad for disturbing him. Because heaven knows how long he's been sitting there, hunched over and hungry. For this prehistoric-looking bird often starves in this severest of seasons. A fact reflected in his screeching call, which is not remotely cutesy, but rather harshly real and primeval.

But more heartbreaking hunting has been happening here. I arrived back from Dublin this day two weeks ago to learn that a fatal accident had taken place the night before. A young man, a neighbour, had fallen into the river.

The hectic sound of helicopters in the early hours broke the devastating news. Everyone commended the gardaí and rescue services for being brilliant.

As was the entire community, which came together. Local businesses provided refreshments for the brave divers and sub-aqua teams who tirelessly trawled the river, and the vast number of volunteers who walked its length.

All were haunted by the loss of a beloved human being, and moved by empathy for his family to find him. Some of those who searched for miles each day had lost loved ones in similar circumstances.

They were there when I drew my curtains each morning, donning wet suits and heaving dinghies down the riverbank, or else setting off once more with walking sticks. They continued their saddest search until dusk, joined in the following days by the Civil Defence, the Army, even the Navy.

The weather was bitterly cold, with numb grey skies to match the mood. Freezing fog descended on the river at night as I stood in my backyard, looking out at the darkness.

A poignant coincidence plagued my mind. For only a few weeks earlier, a friend had sent me *Lycidas,* by 17th century poet John Milton, who is most famous for the epic *Paradise Lost.* A grief-stricken Milton wrote this elegy for his 25-year-old friend Edward King, who drowned on his way home from Ireland.

Then, halfway through day five, they found the missing neighbour. It was the smallest of mercies, I heard people say.

Once more, the riverbank opposite my home was deserted. But the next day I walked its length and came across two candles, encased against the elements, standing opposite the scene of the tragedy.

That evening, I parked on the road parallel to the river. Horse carriers lined the far side. Though dusk had fallen, a hunt was still going on. Not for food to live. Or to find a loved one. But to frighten and kill a little creature in the name of fun.

I thought of the heron, waiting patiently for prey. And I prayed he would soon find them.

No love letter for newly relocated post office

A fresh start is a fine thing. But January is no excuse to nudge out the old – especially if it is the long established core of a community.

And what could be more pivotal to a country town than its post office?

Yet the powers that be apparently consider it progress to push the pulse of this community from its central location into a sideshow in a supermarket on the outskirts of town.

No wonder people looked disorientated when I discovered the lamentable new location. Some feeling the profession of postmaster/postmistress has been stripped of its independent status and identity – like a friend whose straitened circumstances force them to kip on your couch.

And for whose benefit? Surely not locals, who used to cheerfully collide with each other at the post office. For the walk there took you through the heart of this town, passing the butchers (a glance to see if John is wearing his hat today) and Hennessey's B&B next to the eco clothes shop.

Or you might make your way along the opposite side of the road, passing Ted Murphy's and the Indian restaurant, Clay Creations and Vincent's Charity Shop, with its window display always worth a look. Then crossing at O'Hara's on the corner, with its fine Victorian façade and green sash window frames.

You would meet the world and his wife en route to its long-established residence on the quay, for you were likely to pop in and out of these places along the way.

Along with Sim's Hardware or Harmony Health Food Store, The Truffle Fairy chocolate shop; Kissanes across from Healy's Pharmacy, next door to The Salon, with its real fire.

Or you would wander into Woods, beside A-Men barbers, or one of this town's many excellent cafes.

All have succeeded in staying open through the downturns and uproars of the economy. And if I owned one of them, I would be livid with the anonymous authority that seems so detached from the harsh reality of rural Ireland that they have jeopardised their livelihoods by taking away the passing trade that came with the post office.

For any savings are surely at the expense of those independent shopkeepers. Because how many people using the partitioned post office are likely to nip into the supermarket while they're at it?

This is not about sentiment. Or (God forbid!) catering for senior citizens for whom going to the post office was not just about collecting their pension but constituted a social outing. For the new premises presents us with a different kind of uphill walk.

The spirit and sparkle of this country town will also suffer – though that won't show up on any kind of spreadsheet.

Anyway, why shove an essential facility that is used by so many people into a corner of a supermarket when there are so many buildings lying empty? Now there is yet another.

Maybe it's time to post letters of protest that demand: return to sender!

The clash of the clocks in one country town

Maybe it's a personal protest against the powers that be and their penchant for playing God, but it's taken me until today to put my clock back.

I've still arrived where I had to be on time – but only by mentally subtracting an hour when I looked at my watch.

Perhaps this resistance to socially imposed concepts on time – which is itself a construct – is actually a healthy instinct for humans. After all, we're supposed to be smart mammals – not smartphones. (The advent of which have thwarted my tendency by updating automatically.)

Though smartphones could have resolved the fracas that ensued in one Irish town back in 1956, when the issue of Official Summer Time was so explosive that it caused divisions that hadn't been experienced since the Civil War. The only solution was the ballot box.

The fascinating tale is told in *Kilkenny: People, Places, Faces* by John Fitzgerald. It recounts how some employees of State-run services in Callan recognised Summer Time (mainly because they had no choice). So, too, did the bacon factory, a turf accountant, and a number of pubs. But the majority of residents observed Old Time, along with the schools, churches, county council workers and many businesses.

This led to 'chaos and disorder occasioned by the operation of both Old and Official Summer Time,' as a correspondent for a local newspaper wrote.

'Confusion is widespread.'

As if that wasn't bedlam enough, the nearby village of Mullinahone was 25 minutes behind Callan. A cyclist at the time recalled hearing the Angelus ring out three times as he passed through Callan to Mullinahone. Apparently, the latter village observed what is called 'God's Own Time'.

The greatest opposition to change came from farmers, who feared that putting their clocks forward would upset their cows and result in lower milk yields.

This, in turn, created a dilemma for shopkeepers, who could not afford to offend their best customers. The parish priest didn't exactly help matters, not so much sitting on the fence as sanctifying it, by backing the farming community even while emphasising in a sermon that people who observed New Time were not committing a sin.

A referendum day was set to resolve the conflict. But the weeks leading up to it were decidedly bolshie. One public meeting had to be cut short after fistfights broke out between Old Timers and New Timers. Calm was restored only when gardaí arrived and the parish priest intervened.

There were also heated exchanges and fisticuffs in the pubs, and people were often afraid to ask the time.

A huge crowd gathered in the streets to hear the result of the vote. 'The ayes have it,' Superintendent Egan confirmed.

A rousing cheer went up from the 'Yes' camp, as groups of 'No' supporters shook their heads in disbelief.

Less a case of 'time heals all wounds' as time wounds all heels of Johnny-come-lately losers.

Warming up to adventures Down Under

Apparently crime doesn't pay. But for the first Irish convicts who arrived in New South Wales, Australia, on this day back in 1791 *(26th November)*, at least punishment brought the consolation prize of warmer climes.

No wonder it's pleasure and not penance that has Paddies actually paying to go Down Under these days. Some never return, especially since social media makes it possible to stay virtually in touch with loved ones on the old sod.

But plenty more view an adventure in Australia as a rite of passage rather than a permanent destination, combining work experience with decent pay and all the exotic extras that come with long distance travel. While the savvy try to time their trip so they can steal themselves a second summer.

Like Katie, the petite powerhouse who works in the convenience store on the main street of this country town.

She is only in her early twenties but has common sense in spades and her head firmly on her shoulders. Katie always has a kind word for everyone who enters this treasure trove of trivia, no matter whether she's busy stocking shelves, buttering breakfast rolls or serving ice-cream sundaes to kids who seem to think we're enjoying Australia's current temperatures.

But right now, Katie is 'all over the place, trying to get sorted' before she heads to Australia for a month's break.

A major part of her preparation is not what she's packing but leaving behind: her dogs PJ and his Mrs Mutt, Phoebe; along with their three daughters, Maxi, Rose and Phoenix, who Katie also adopted when it became clear that nobody else was going to offer them a home.

And forget Mary with her lonesome lamb, for Katie also has two fleecy friends, Sean and Shirley, along with a cat called Thomas and 13-year-old Toby, the geriatric goldfish.

At least her boss, Catherine, understands the fussing for the voyage, for some of her children have been living in Australia for years.

But it's not just young guns that can hack the considerable hike involved in getting there – as Catherine discovered when her 80-year-old mother asked if she would accompany her on a visit to see her two sisters, who were both nuns.

Catherine agreed, thinking that she was joking. But the next day her mother started looking into flights and visas. Till next thing Catherine knew, they were fastening their seat belts and on their way to the other side of the world.

The aunts promised to spoil them and offered free accommodation. No wonder Catherine had fantasies of hanging out in hammocks and eating Bounty bars for breakfast.

Which was a far cry from the convent dormitory that awaited her, single beds separated from each other by what looked like hospital curtains.

Leaving Catherine feeling like she was doing time, instead of having a good one.

And guilty of being very glad to escape back home.

Dashed against the rocks, but never say die

We are three weeks and one day into the new year – and hence well ensconced in winter. But some folk go further than lighting a candle instead of cursing the darkness. Like Canice Hogan, who has lit up a tree outside his magnificent old mill on this country town's waterfront, so it glows like a ghost ship at night.

Certainly, stormy weather may wreak havoc on land – but it is especially lethal at sea, turning waves into weapons of destruction. My tales last week about shipwrecks off the tiny but treacherous Keeragh Islands pale in comparison to the worst disasters that happen at sea. Though tragedy was matched by heroism in one case I have in mind, which remains one of the greatest rescue operations ever undertaken off the Irish coast.

It happened on February 20, 1914, when the Norwegian schooner *Mexico* was driven into Bannow Bay in a bad south-south-west gale and lost her bearings. Captain Eriksen described 'mountain-high waves' as they were approaching the South Keeragh Islands.

Her plight was spotted in Fethard, where the lifeboat *Helen Blake* set out to help. It was just a few hundred yards from the infamous islands when Garrett Handrick recalled three 'terrible waves'.

The first filled the boat; the second struck her with terrible force; while the third toppled the crew from the vessel.

Fellow crew member John McNamara was swirled about in the breakers before being caught by a tremendous wave and dashed towards an alcove in the cliff. Here, he managed to grab Handrick by a hook on his lifebelt.

'Handrick shouted out to me to let him go and save myself if I could,' McNamara remembered. 'I answered: "I suppose they are all gone now but the two of us – and we will go or come together". '

Indeed, only five of the 14 crew members made it ashore. Yet those brave men then set about rescuing the crew of the *Mexico* and soon had all nine safely off the schooner and on the island.

But they were still in deep water. From Friday until Monday, the 14 survivors huddled on the gale-swept isle as attempts to rescue them failed.

One of the *Mexico's* crew died from exposure on Sunday and his body was covered with canvas and sods.

The remaining 13 knew they faced certain death unless rescuers came soon. They had nothing to eat except two small tins of preserved meat and raw limpets. Their only drink was a little brandy and half a pint of wine, plus rainwater pooling in the alcoves.

On Monday morning, the Dunmore East lifeboat managed to rescue two men.

Then the Rosslare lifeboat got close enough for James Wickham and William Duggan to drag two more aboard their punt – before it was flung against rocks and holed. They hastily plugged the gap with a loaf of bread inside some packing and made four more hazardous trips to rescue the remaining men.

Thereby saving the day by defying the darkness.

Southpaws of the world, right is on your side

It's the season for sniffles, but thankfully the only coughing up I did recently was for a check up with the doctor in this country town. Una, the receptionist, wrote me out a receipt afterwards – though not with the hand that roughly 90% of the world's population uses.

'I'm a leftie,' she confirmed cheerfully.

Being left-handed is no big deal for Una – but, unfortunately, it was for one of the nuns who taught her at school. Sewing was Una's favourite subject – until this nun forced her to do it with her right hand. The experience killed Una's love for sewing.

But Una reckons she got off lightly compared with the left-handed boy she knew back then who had the most beautiful handwriting.

'They beat and beat his left hand and made him write with the right one,' Una remembers. He still does – in an ugly, spidery scrawl.

Yet even in this day and age of supposed equality, left-handers still have to live in a right-handed world. From scissors to corkscrews and playing cards to pens – even modern technology designs apps for right-handers and locates buttons on the right side of computers so your left hand blocks the screen.

Because if might is right, it seems right is doubly so. Even the word 'dexterity' reveals a right-handed bias, where 'dexter' means 'right' and refers to being 'right-handed' on both sides.

Which is hardly surprising, when left-handedness has traditionally been viewed as everything from a mark of the devil, to a sign of illness and criminality.

Prejudice is embedded in the word itself, with 'sinister' the Latin word for 'left'. This is echoed in English, where it comes from the term for 'weak' or 'broken'.

It's no better here, with the Irish for left-handed – 'ciotóg' – all too close to 'ciotach', meaning 'clumsy', as well as having connotations as 'the strange one'.

Even the Eskimos viewed left-handers as potential sorcerors.

Perhaps this stigma plays a part in why left-handers are more likely to be dyslexic and to stutter. As Una's experience illustrates, many were persecuted in school, where they were forced to write with their right hand and sometimes beaten if they did so badly. Others were made to sit on their left hand.

And while there are saints assigned to everything from abdominal pain to tax collectors, not a single one laments the lot of left-handers.

Though it doesn't look like they need it, as being left-handed can indicate creativity and high intelligence. It certainly didn't hurt Albert Einstein, Isaac Newton or Charles Darwin.

Left-handers now celebrate being left field on August 13. And while you might think it's because Mullingar is located in the midlands (thus allowing it to eschew right and left) that led it to host The Left Hand Festival in 2013, the real reason is because 'Mullingar' translates as 'the town of the left-hand mill', after a miraculous seventh-century legend.

Because when two wrongs don't make a right, the truth is all that's left.

Remembering the mother of matriarchs

This cold November wind is a far cry from the balmy breeze that blew me into a West Cork shop last summer, where a piece by artist Etain Hickey caught my eye.

'Pray for the dead. Fight like hell for the living' was inscribed above an image of a middle-aged woman, stoutly dressed in dark coat and hat, wearing round glasses and carrying the sort of handbag that old ladies use to bash hooligans in comic skits.

But it made sense when I saw it was Mother Jones, who played a key role in the man's world of union and mining politics of turn-of-the-century America.

Barely five foot tall, she controlled 'her boys' with a glance of her sharp, steel-grey eyes.

'My father was an Irish refugee,' she used to say, referring to the Famine that forced her family to emigrate from Cork in the early 1850s, 'and I think some of his rebellious blood must linger in my veins.'

Along with the many contradictions that led Freud to say the Irish could not be pyschoanalysed. Like the fact that she stood up for the rights of men, but believed a woman's place was in the home. And was childless, yet famously known as a mother.

Though horrendous suffering lay behind that latter riddle. For Mary Harris Jones was indeed a mother – until yellow fever struck in 1867. 'One by one, my four little children sickened and died,' she later wrote. 'I washed their little bodies and got them ready for burial. My husband caught the fever and died. I sat alone through nights of grief.'

But within four years, she was back on her feet and had built up a dressmaking business – only to lose everything in the 1871 Great Fire of Chicago.

Leading her to epitomise what doesn't kill you makes you stronger – and become a thorn in the side of the establishment in the process. For she reinvented herself to become a mighty matriarch of the American labour movement.

Nor could age wither this lethal weapon of a woman, who was in her 70s when she was dubbed the 'most dangerous woman in America'.

So it's ironic that the so-called 'great grandchildren of Mother Jones' became Donald Trump's most staunch supporters.

Though she was fond of utilising the fake news that has come to characterise his presidency. She was born in August 1837 but claimed her birthday was seven years earlier on Labour Day, apparently to enhance her radical credentials. While she donned old-fashioned dresses and whitened her hair to add to her image as a wise old woman.

Which is how Mary Harris Jones managed to pass away next Friday *(November 30)* in 1830 at the age of 93 – six months after celebrating her 100th birthday.

'My address is like my shoes. It travels with me,' this formidable female once declared. 'I abide where there is a fight against wrong.'

Trump had better hope an east wind doesn't blow this Mary Poppins of the proletariat into the White House.

Something about Mary in face-off with felons

'Sisters are doin' it for themselves,' sang Annie Lennox and Aretha Franklin back in 1985, in a duet that was widely regarded as a modern feminist anthem.

And while it's not unusual to see women in positions of power nowadays, it's still heartening to hear about a damsel in distress 'standin' on her own two feet'.

Especially when she's doing so half-naked, before a gang of gurriers who have broken into her home.

It happened last month to Mary, who lives in a pretty village nearby. She shares her home with her girlfriend, who she is set to marry in a civil ceremony later this year.

Their love nest is in a row of period houses nestled in the heart of the community, making it feel secure. So the fact that it was targeted for a break-in should act as a warning that not only isolated abodes are in danger of losing their domestic bliss. Complacency could cuckold you, for nowhere is safe from the travelling gangs that are still terrorising rural Ireland.

This despite the considerable efforts of Operation Fiacla, set up two years ago next month to combat a wave of brutal burglaries (*Operation Fiacla was set up in 2012.*) Latest figures show a 9% decrease in break-ins and a 13% rise in incidents catching those intent on burglaries. But the bad news is that this crime continues to blight the countryside.

Gangs are often armed with shotguns and drive high-powered stolen cars, allowing them to use the motorways to carry out their crimes. They regularly commit up to 12 burglaries across a number of counties in one trip.

This particular posse had been watching Mary's modest home. They had seen her girlfriend leave that afternoon and decided to wreak havoc.

It was teatime when Mary got in from work and decided to have a shower. So she went into the bathroom. She had almost stripped off, when in burst two men armed with crowbars.

Mary screamed. Then, without thinking, she charged at them.

Perhaps the shock of seeing this mere slip of a thing hurtling their way startled the men into fleeing outside, where a third man was waiting in a car.

But they didn't get a chance to climb in, as Mary gave chase in her nearly altogether, roaring blue murder till her neighbours came out to help.

Finally the gang sped off. But the gardaí caught them later.

So I don't know if 'behind every great man, there had to be a great woman'. But 'the fair sex' seems well capable these days of getting in the face of a few felons.

Still learning before this year is left behind

They say 'you learn something new every day'. Then again, the exasperated expression 'will I ever learn?' is equally popular.

Which is perhaps something to consider, given we are four days from a new year's blank slate. For many of us will fill it with rehashed versions of resolutions that have come – and just as swiftly gone – before.

Anyone who moves to a new neck of the woods, with all its new mores, especially has a lot to learn. So, as a city slicker who upped sticks to the sticks several years ago, I'm probably guiltier than most of falling between those two conflicting stools.

But I did learn something new this Christmas.

I was giving the place a quick sweep before retiring one night, when I looked down by the fridge and couldn't quite believe my eyes. Though this was partly due to the lackadaisical lights in this town cottage – they have a life of their own, made worse by a dysfunctional dimmer, frequently resulting in a slapstick scenario; whereby you switch them on, only to find yourself in near darkness again by the time you've entered the kitchen.

So it took me a while to realise that the shadow on the floor was in fact a body. A small body, I grant you, but a body nonetheless. And indeed, a furry one, two legs ending in feet with accompanying tail.

I was deeply disturbed by this macabre discovery. Because aside from the frightful fact that there was a dead mouse in the house, he seemed a strangely oversized specimen.

I wondered if perhaps he was not recently deceased, and hence bloated from decomposition? Or could he in fact be a rat that my Deputy Dawg had dredged up from the river that flows just behind our yard?

However, he was just too massive to be a mouse. Yet, Goldilocks style, he seemed too small for a rat, even a runt.

Plus, he was a riddle for other reasons. Because in a reversal of that Red Riding Hood scene, where she notices what big ears her granny has, his were way too small.

'Hmm,' I thought, sage as Sherlock Holmes.

'Humm,' I appended, as I considered his terribly short tail.

To cap it all, his reddish brown coat was a conundrum, as neither rodent has that colouring.

Perhaps it was the effect of my lighting, for it took me ages to have the bright idea of checking a wildlife reference book. I skimmed past the slugs and flicked by our feathered friends, till suddenly I spied a spitting image of the little mystery man lying flat out on my floor.

So for a while I admired what was actually a bank vole – from his benign expression and closed eyes, to his neatly folded little elfin ears. I've no idea what killed him. But I am now certain that you do indeed 'live and learn', even if just occasionally.

Because I've realised that it's still possible to put the words 'benign' and 'bank' in the same sentence.

Variety both the spice of life and future of farming

We are one day from completing the first week of the fresh start known as a new year.

Though climate change doesn't care about calendar dates. So it's heartening to hear that some agricultural folk are also a step ahead when it comes to rural resolutions, with 'Farming for Nature' holding its inaugural awards last autumn.

This inspiring initiative respects the connection between our survival and that of insects, birds and other wildlife.

Though not only farmers need to forge new relations and recognise the link between choices and consequences. Christmas may have literally had its day but isn't over yet – and not just in terms of tinsel trees and lights still twinkling around this country town. For the mindset of insane spending at the cheapest price persists.

So I was reminded when I nipped into New Ross, one of those under-the-radar yet resilient towns that are a credit to this country.

Free parking encouraged consumers to splash the cash and allowed me take a break in 'The Nutshell' to enjoy its brilliant bedlam and buzz over a mug of coffee depicting a robin wearing a woolly hat. That sort of attention to detail probably explains why there were queues out the door.

The owners were full of Christmas cheer, despite a 16-hour day because their baker had a family emergency.

'It had to be done,' Philip shrugged. 'People were depending on us.'

Like their staff depend on the dynamic duo all year round, as do their local suppliers.

Ultimately, they all depend on us to support these businesses that give country towns their character.

Yet some say that cosy cafes and shops with surnames are too expensive. Even though, as a business owner in this town points out, they go to the chipper most nights.

'Takeaways need to make a living,' she adds. 'But some people eat there all the time, yet then say they can't afford a meal in a family restaurant.'

She shops in supermarkets too but tries to make sure that she 'spreads it around.' Which is why the brussels sprouts for her festive dinner came in a paper bag that had the farmer's name on it.

'It's a vicious circle,' she says. 'People buy vegetables in the supermarket because it's so cheap but end up throwing out loads. Whereas if you buy good quality, the farmer gets paid properly, the land is looked after, and you value the food.'

Plus it's more fun buying in shops that are 'real local' as she puts it. Her husband figured they only needed 10 minutes to pick up some items recently but it actually took ages because they were chatting with the staff and generally having a laugh.

'We need lots of quirky little places,' Patsy of 'The Nutshell' agrees. 'People want real shops run by families and individuals.'

For variety is not just the spice of life but the key to our future.

Backing small businesses linked to farmers who support biodiversity needs to become the norm and not niche to really nail this being a genuinely new year.

Why birthdays are not the only new beginnings

It's the eve of New Year's Eve; meaning time is running out for 2018. Maybe it's telling that younger folk generally view the year's end as an excuse to party. Whereas the older we get, the more we tend to batten down the hatches and just get through it.

Perhaps we see the parallels between the dying year and our own mortality; breathing a sigh of relief with the birth of a new year after the frantic fuss over the passing of the previous one.

Though some people tidily come full circle when they shuffle off their mortal coil; like the creative genius who coined that phrase. For it is said that Shakespeare was born and died on the same day.

While John Adams and Thomas Jefferson – the second and third presidents of the United States of America – took things a step further by passing away on the same day exactly 50 years after the Declaration of Independence was signed.

They were such great friends that the last words of 90-year-old Adams were supposedly: 'Thomas Jefferson still survives'. Though he was wrong about that, Jefferson having taken his leave five hours earlier, at the age of 82.

Back to birthdays, with the most common months to make your appearance being May, September and October.

While more babies are born on a Tuesday than any other day – unless it falls on Christmas Day, that is. For the least common birthdays – after the leap year of February 29 – is St Stephen's Day followed by Christmas Day. So a birthday this season makes you special.

Perhaps that's the consolation prize for getting joint Christmas and birthday presents – if anyone remembers your birthday at all.

It's hardly surprising that we prefer fresh starts to the angst that can accompany *Auld Lang Syne,* especially as few of us are in any hurry to find out for sure if there is a hereafter.

Though reflecting on the fact that we know our birthday – but not the one that will turn out to be our death day, so to speak, could help us make the most of them all.

Because whatever awaits us in the new year ahead, the big question is whether there is more to come after our package holiday on planet Earth ends.

Emanuel Swedenborg, the theologian and scientist who lived during the Enlightenment, believed that 'absolutely everything (in heaven) appears in its loveliest springtime and its loveliest bloom, with stunning magnificence and variety'.

He added that 'almost all the people who arrive from this world are astonished as they can be to find that they are alive and just as human as ever'.

In particular, atheists are 'profoundly embarrassed' to discover they still exist, despite having exited stage left.

Making funerals surely the ultimate surprise party, where we get to witness our loved ones toasting our memory.

Then again, many of us are so sick from festive celebrations by the time the new year arrives that we feel (if not look, hopefully) like death warmed up. And all too happy to hibernate, before emerging anew in the spring.

Don't fall out with 'feathered apes' of skies

'As far as the crow flies,' so the saying goes. Which is arguably the best way to view these most common of birds. Especially in the evenings, when they form black clouds in the skies.

But popularity shouldn't make crows appear commonplace. Because whatever about 'where eagles dare,' surely marching around motorways proves the mettle – or madness – of these jet-black Jezabels.

I have seen crows hanging lifelessly from a rope outside a field. Some farmers are so frustrated by them chomping on their crops that they capture one alive, to make not so much a scarecrow, as a sorry scapegoat out of them.

Yet these cawing cadgers cannot help trying – and often succeeding – in outsmarting us. For crows are no bird-brains. A test in 2004 revealed that crows are cleverer than some chimps – leading scientists to dub them 'feathered apes'.

Indeed, crows have been known to change their entire migration pattern in order to avoid farms where a single crow has been killed. Generations later, they still remember specific houses where a bird died.

This was illustrated in Ontario, Canada, when over half a million crows began using the farming community of Chatham as a rest stop along their migratory route.

War was declared on the black beggars. But word spreads fast in crow circles. The first day the hunters went out, they shot only one crow. Because after that, the crows made sure to fly high enough to avoid getting hit.

But tread carefully if you fancy picking a fight with these feathered apes. For crows not only remember your face but can conspire against you, as researchers in Seattle discovered.

They captured seven crows, while wearing masks. After they released them, the crows remembered the masks and attacked whenever they saw them. If the researchers wore different masks, the crows left them alone. But as soon as they put the offending masks back on, the crows dive-bombed them again.

Those who get the heebie-jeebies watching Alfred Hitchcock's *The Birds* better skip the next bit. Because the researchers then realised that all the crows in the area acted aggressively towards them when they were wearing the masks.

As a result of this finding, it is now common for people working with wild crows to wear disguises when capturing them, in order to avoid attacks later in life.

Yet crows can be kind when they experience the same from human kind. One woman who works with crows at a wild care facility in the States insists that they are 'such sweet, smart birds'. She feeds the local crows and says they know the exact time that she leaves for work, perching nearby to wait. 'They gift me feathers, shells and trinkets on my porch,' she adds.

No need to crow about it.

Shrill screams greet the seasonal squatters

Halloween seems a distant memory, though in reality it's less than a fortnight since that fright night. Few children live on our road, so I rarely get little callers knocking on my door.

But there are plenty of other cute creatures knocking on my walls. For it seems I'm not the only one who prefers dryness to damp, as I've discovered, with the arrival of the first autumnal mouse in the house.

My parents used death traps to deal with these insignificantly sized imposters. I remember one poor fellow broke his back in one. My father flushed him down the toilet, which at least put him out of his misery.

Some people laugh at live traps, saying the mice just come back. But I take them a good distance; in case the mini-mastermind within has left a trail of crumbs. If the occasional maverick retraces his steps, I applaud his sense of direction, before promptly evicting him again.

I got rid of 20 little grey gatecrashers this way last year. Even if it was the same sneaky squatter, so what? Because when it comes to the question of mice and men, or mice and me, I'd rather remove them than make them prematurely meet their maker.

But I must be out of practice after our long summer, because when this particular pest made his presence felt recently, it caught me unawares.

I heard noises in the kitchen, where I found Mister Mighty Mouse bounding along the wall behind the cooker. Leading me to let out a scream best reserved for an X-rated horror movie.

Mister Mighty took nifty note and duly disappeared. But that didn't put me at pest-free ease. I kept turning down the TV whenever I heard, not a 'puddy tat', as 'Tweety Pie' might say, which would have been handy in the circumstances, but another of his unfortunate objects of affection.

So I placed a baited live trap in the bathroom, where it wasn't long before I heard a noise. I crept upstairs to find the trap shut and rocking with a vengeance, accompanied by the sound of desperate clawing.

My little hostage went hush-hush as I carried him over the bridge and down the floodplain, where he charged off into the night as soon as I released him.

Some mice cower even after you open the trap, so I felt sure this energetic inmate was the same one I had seen doing the mini marathon over my mixing bowls.

The trap was shut again the next morning; I took it to the floodplain but it was empty. It was shut again later but felt lifeless and light, so I opened it in the bathroom. Out sprang a mortified mouse. Cue my second blood-curdling scream in 24 hours.

The trap is rattling once more as I write. If only one click of my computer mouse could erase the spooky sound!